baby says sew

20 Practical, Budget-Minded, Baby-Approved Projects

Rebecca Danger

Martingale
Create with Confidence

Baby Says Sew: 20 Practical, Budget-Minded,
Baby-Approved Projects
© 2014 by Rebecca Danger

Martingale®
19021 120th Ave. NE, Ste. 102
Bothell, WA 98011-9511 USA
ShopMartingale.com

Printed in China
19 18 17 16 15 14   8 7 6 5 4 3 2 1

Library of Congress Cataloging-in-Publication Data
is available upon request.

ISBN: 978-1-60468-423-0

MISSION STATEMENT
Dedicated to providing quality products and service to inspire creativity.

CREDITS

PUBLISHER AND CHIEF VISIONARY OFFICER: Jennifer Erbe Keltner

EDITOR IN CHIEF: Mary V. Green

DESIGN DIRECTOR: Paula Schlosser

MANAGING EDITOR: Karen Costello Soltys

ACQUISITIONS EDITOR: Karen M. Burns

TECHNICAL EDITOR: Laurie Baker

COPY EDITOR: Marcy Heffernan

PRODUCTION MANAGER: Regina Girard

COVER DESIGNER: Paula Schlosser

INTERIOR DESIGNER: Adrienne Smitke

PHOTOGRAPHER: Brent Kane

ILLUSTRATOR: Christine Erikson

CONTENTS

INTRODUCTION

Hello and welcome to my very first sewing book! I cannot even begin to tell you how excited I am about this book.

I've been sewing since I was a very little girl. I started by making toys and doll clothes on my mom's old Kenmore sewing machine, but that process never went very well because it took me a long time to figure out what a seam allowance was. Fast-forward a few years to high school, and I convinced my neighbor to officially teach me to sew. This meant instead of going out and partying on the weekends like other kids, I stayed home and made stuff. At 19 I used my newfound skill set to launch my first business, making handbags. I ran my business for more than seven years, at the height of which I worked full-time along with my husband, had five employees, and occupied a 3000-square-foot manufacturing/warehouse/retail space. I ended up closing my sewing business because I burned myself out, and I began writing knitting patterns instead. I found my passion writing patterns. At the release of this book, I've authored three knitting books and published more than 100 knitting patterns.

Sewing has been such a huge and important part of my life that when I found out I was pregnant with my son Presley, it was only natural I'd make as much for him as I could. As I got back into sewing again, I realized I loved writing sewing patterns as much as knitting patterns and began to release a few sewing patterns. So, when the opportunity to write a nursery sewing book came up, it seemed like such a great and natural way to expand on my love of writing patterns that I jumped at the chance.

The best thing about this book is that I originally made these projects for my son when he was born. We used them throughout his first two years before I actually wrote down a single instruction. That means I tested everything I made as a new mama, and then used my experiences to tweak the designs to create the patterns for this book. I also added in a few patterns for things I would want to have if I were to do it all again. And, since I found out I was pregnant with our second baby while writing this book, what I would want was in my thoughts all the time!

I've rated the skill level of each of these projects by how many nap times it would take to get the project finished—from one to three nap times. A single nap-time rating (Super Easy) is a simple project that even a beginning sewist could tackle. Two nap-time projects are Easy, and three nap times (Intermediate) require a little more experience. Each project is noted with its skill level and indicated with one to three napping baby illustrations.

Being a mom is the most challenging, and rewarding, experience of my life. Whether you're expecting your first, second, or tenth baby, or you have a special little person in your life, I hope that what I've learned and can share with you in these projects will help you add both fun and function to your precious time with baby.

Happy sewing,

Rebecca

Turtle Stacker

I adore the classic ring stacker for babies. Ironically, Presley never had one! I decided to jazz up the classic a little bit, but what could be cooler than a stack of rings? Some type of animal for sure. I thought long and hard about which animals would stack well and I decided turtles were it. They're nice and round and have little limbs that are perfect for baby to explore (and chew on, of course!). I know babies and toddlers will love the repetition of the turtle in different sizes and that they stick together when stacked. If you don't want to make the complete set, an individual turtle makes an excellent toy. Try filling the turtles with polystyrene beads instead of a stuffing like fiberfill for a floppy throwing toy. I know your kiddo will get a ton of play out of this thing.

FINISHED SIZES (head to tail)
Extra small: 7⅜", Small: 11¾", Medium: 15¼", Large: 18⅝", Extra large: 22½"

SKILL LEVEL

Easy

MATERIALS

Approximately 12 fat quarters (18" x 21") of quilting cotton in various colors and prints (amount will depend on color-mixing preference)

12" of 1½"-wide sew-on Velcro

Stuffing

Black puffy fabric paint for eyes (optional)

Hand-sewing needle and thread to match fat quarters

PATTERN NOTES

◆ Patterns for all turtle pieces are on pullout pattern sheet 1.

◆ All seam allowances are ¼" and are included in the pattern pieces unless otherwise noted.

◆ Wash, dry, and iron all fabrics before cutting out the pieces.

CUTTING

For *each* size turtle, cut:*
2 body pieces
2 tail pieces
2 head pieces
8 leg pieces

*Mix and match colors and prints for each turtle as desired or refer to the photo on page 6 for ideas.

INSTRUCTIONS

Sew all pieces right sides together using a ¼" seam allowance unless otherwise noted.

1. Sew the Heads, Legs, and Tails

Place each head, leg, and tail piece together with another piece of the same shape and size and sew the pieces together around the outer edges, leaving an opening for turning and stuffing where indicated on the patterns. Clip into the seam allowances along the curved edges of the head and leg pieces, and then turn all of the pieces, including the tails, to the right side. Stuff each piece using a blunt tool, such as a chopstick, to push the stuffing to the outer edges and smooth out the curves. Leave about ½" of space at the opening, and be sure not to overstuff the pieces or they'll be hard to attach to the body later.

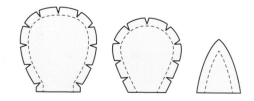

2. Attach the Velcro to the Bodies

Cut four 2"-long pieces of Velcro.

Velcro placement will depend on which turtle in the stack you're working on. The top (extra-small) turtle gets a piece of hook tape on the body bottom piece *only*, and the bottom (extra-large) turtle gets a piece of loop tape on the body top piece *only*. If you want to be able to stack your turtles in any order, you can add Velcro to both the top and bottom pieces of all the turtles.

For each turtle, fold both body circles in half vertically and horizontally and press the folds to mark the centers. Unfold the pieces. Center a loop (soft) piece of the Velcro on the right side of the top circle (except for the extra-small turtle) and a hook piece on the right side of the bottom circle (except for the extra-large turtle). Sew each piece of Velcro in place, sewing as close to the edge of the tape as possible. If you want to, trim across each corner of the Velcro to angle the corners and remove the pokey corners.

3. Attach the Limbs to the Bodies

Using the fold lines on each turtle for reference, center and pin the tail on one of the fold lines of the bottom body circle, aligning the raw edges. Center and pin the head to the opposite end of the same fold line, aligning the raw edges. Center and pin each leg in one of the quarters created by the fold lines, aligning the raw edges. Baste the pieces in place, about ⅛" from the edges.

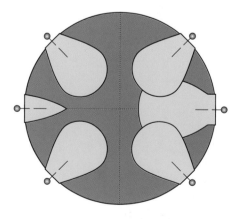

4. Sew the Bodies

For each turtle, pin the body top circle to the body bottom circle. Be sure the head, legs, and tail are facing inward and trapped between the two layers. Beginning near one back leg and using a ⅜" seam allowance, sew around the body to just the tail side of the other back leg. Leave the tail section between the two back legs open for turning. Be sure you've caught all the limbs in the stitching.

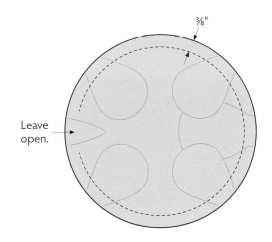

⅜"

Leave open.

5. Finish the Turtles

Turn each turtle right side out and stuff. Sculpt the shell as you stuff, and once it looks right, grab another handful of stuffing and stick it in the top center to bring the shell up a little higher. With a needle and thread that matches the turtle fabric, use a ladder stitch (page 94) to close the tail section.

Now, get stacking!

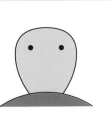 **THE EYES HAVE IT**

If you want eyes, use puffy paint and apply two dots to the top of the head. Practice making the eyes on a piece of scrap fabric first.

Super Bear

While I was pregnant with my son Presley, I happened across one of those blanket toys that was a superhero bear. Being a sucker for anything superhero, I really wanted to buy it. But, I also felt like I'd had my wallet out since becoming pregnant—babies sure can be expensive. I finally decided I would kick myself if I passed up this super friend. Good thing I bought him—he quickly became and stayed one of Presley's favorite toys. He is so well loved in our house that I included my very own version of Super Bear in this book.

FINISHED SIZE
Approximately 20" tall

SKILL LEVEL

Easy

MATERIALS

1 yard of 54"-wide ultra-plush fleece for bear body

1 fat quarter (18" x 21") of quilting cotton for cape

½ yard *OR* 1 fat quarter of flannel-backed satin for cape lining

7" x 7" square of contrasting fleece or felt for mask band and cape band

Small piece of black fleece or felt for eyes and nose

PATTERN NOTES

◆ Patterns for all bear and cape pieces are on pullout pattern sheet 2.

◆ All seam allowances are ¼" and are included in the pattern pieces unless otherwise noted.

◆ Wash, dry, and iron all fabrics using the appropriate temperature settings before cutting out the pieces.

CUTTING

From the ultra-plush fleece, cut:
2 body pieces

From the quilting cotton, cut:
1 cape piece

From the flannel-backed satin, cut:
1 cape piece

From the contrasting fleece or felt, cut:
1 mask piece
1 mask band piece
2 cape band pieces

From the black fleece or felt, cut:
2 eye pieces
1 nose piece

2. Sew the Mask to the Body Front

Designate one body piece as the body front and the other as the body back. With right sides up, pin the mask in place on the right side of the body front, using the marks on the pattern as a guide. Using a zigzag stitch with a narrow width and medium length, stitch around the outer edges of the mask, catching the mask with the zig and the body with the zag. Do the same for the eye openings. Pin and stitch the remaining cape band to the neck as indicated on the pattern and stitch it in place in the same manner.

3. Sew the Mask and Cape to the Body Back

Using the mask marks as a guide, pin the mask band to the body back and stitch it in place as you did for the front. Stitch the cape band in place on the body back in the same manner, making sure the band will align with the front band and stitching through both the band and cape along the cape top edge.

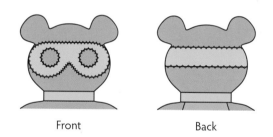

Front   Back

INSTRUCTIONS

Sew all pieces right sides together using a ¼" seam allowance unless otherwise noted.

1. Sew the Cape

Sew the cape and cape lining pieces together around the side and bottom edges, leaving the top edges open as indicated on the pattern. Clip the seam allowances of the rounded corners. Turn the cape to the right side and press the edges. Topstitch the finished edges of the cape, stitching about ⅛" from the edges. With the wrong side of the cape band facing the right side of the cape front, center the band over the top edge, overlapping the edges about ½". Baste the band to the cape.

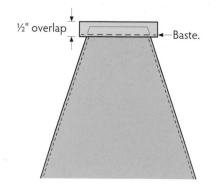

½" overlap   Baste.

4. Stitch the Face

Transfer the mouth line to the bear face, starting under where the nose is placed so that the ends of the stitching will be covered when the nose is stitched in place. Set your machine for a wide zigzag stitch width and a narrow stitch length. Using black thread, stitch over the mouth lines. Pin the nose and eyes in place and zigzag stitch around them in the same manner as you did for the mask and bands.

5. Pin the Body Together

Roll up the cape and pin it to the body to keep it out of the way for this step. Pin the body pieces together. Ultra-plush fleece, such as Minky, is slippery; use a lot of pins. Sew around the body pieces, starting and stopping where indicated on the pattern.

6. Trim and Turn the Body

Clip into the seam allowances up to but not through the stitching line at inside points and rounded corners of the body pieces to help them lie flat once turned: armpits, around ears, neck, hands, feet, ears, etc. Also, clip into the thick part where the fleece mask and cape bands are sewn to the face to help the layers lie flatter once turned. Turn the body right side out, using a chopstick to push out the corners and smooth the curves.

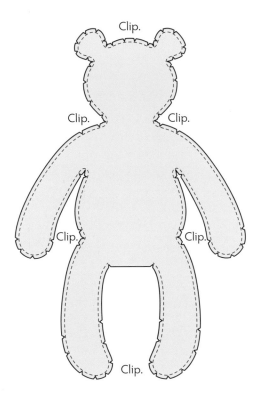

7. Finish Your Super Friend

Fold under the raw edge ¼" at the bear opening and topstitch along the edge. This is a texture toy and it is intentionally left unstuffed. Set your iron on low and use it to press the seams. Tie a knot in the arms and legs about 1½" up from the ends. To be sure they're even, knot one leg and use it as a reference when knotting the second leg. Repeat for the arms.

Go find a kiddo in need of a Super Buddy. This should be quite easy as *all* kiddos are in need of a Super Buddy!

GET CREATIVE!

The whole point of this guy is to give baby textures to explore. I encourage you to go to the fabric store and pick out as many different textured fabrics as you can find to make your Super Bear. You could do the cape bands in a different fabric, or even make the back of the bear different from the front. Explore with your fingers and make this guy your own! Just double-check that the fabrics you pick are machine washable (because this toy will need to be washed many, many times).

Super Bear also looks good without the superhero mask and cape. Or, stuff him for a whole different toy!

No superhero friend is complete without a cape!

Taggie Blocks

I made a blankie with ribbon tags on it for Presley when he was born. He liked it well enough, but I think he would have enjoyed it more if it had been a three-dimensional item, rather than a flat blanket. So here's my version: a block with ribbon tags on it. He's always loved stacking things, so I'm sure these would have been a hit when he was little.

These blocks require only small amounts of fabric, so you can make them using scraps from other projects. I recommend lots of bold black-and-white graphics, because that's what babies like. Add more ribbons if you wish—I used just a few for texture, but I also added bells, squeakers, rattles, and crinkles. Whatever you do, this toy is sure to be a handful of fun from infancy up to when throwing things becomes the favorite toddler activity!

FINISHED SIZE
5" cube

SKILL LEVEL

Super Easy

MATERIALS (for 1 block)

6 squares, 5½" x 5½", of assorted cotton prints*

½ yard of ⅞"-wide or wider ribbon

Stuffing

Noisemakers for inside (see "Resources," page 95)

Hand-sewing needle and matching thread

Use fabric leftovers, fat quarters, or whatever you have on hand.

PATTERN NOTES

◆ All seam allowances are ¼" and are included in the cut sizes unless otherwise noted.

◆ Wash, dry, and iron all fabrics before cutting out the pieces.

CUTTING

From the ribbon, cut:
4 pieces, 4" long

INSTRUCTIONS

Sew all pieces right sides together using a ¼" seam allowance unless otherwise noted. Press the seam allowances open.

1. Sew on the Ribbon Tags

Select one 5½" fabric square for the top of the block and one square for the bottom of the block. Fold each square in half and press the fold. Fold each ribbon in half widthwise and press the fold. With the raw edges aligned, center and pin each ribbon at the ends of the fold lines; baste in place about ⅛" from the edge.

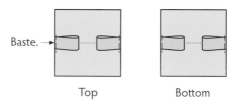

Top   Bottom

2. Sew the Squares into a Cross

Sew a square without ribbon loops to each loop side of the square you designated for the top of the block, beginning and ending the stitching line ¼" from the ends and backstitching at each end. Repeat on the remaining sides of the top square. Add the square you designated for the bottom of the block to the square you sewed to the bottom edge of the top square, attaching it along a ribbon-loop edge.

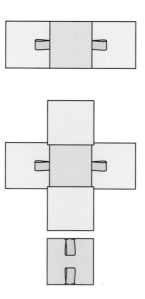

3. Sew Three Sides Together

Sew the top and bottom edges of the two side squares to the sides of the squares sewn above and below the "top" square. Sew the first pair of edges, starting at the seam end and stopping ¼" from the unsewn end; backstitch at the beginning and end of the stitching line. Repeat for the remaining side square.

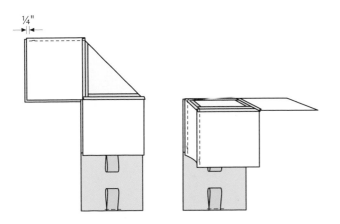

4. Sew the Remaining Side

Working on the final open side, pin the three seams together to form the cube. Sew the two side seams as you did in step 3. Then, starting at the edge, sew about 1" of the final seam, lift your presser foot and needle, leave about 2" to 3" unstitched so you can turn the block to the right side later, and begin sewing again; sew all the way to the edge. You'll finish this seam later.

5. Finish the Block

Turn the block right side out through the opening in the final seam. Stuff the block and add any bells, squeakers, or crinkle material now. Use a ladder stitch (page 94) to hand sew the opening closed.

Find a kid, and stack (or toss) some blocks!

Soft Toy Bin

When Presley was still a little guy and just mobile enough to get toys out of his toy box, we had a basket that we kept everything in. He'd reach with all his might to the bottom of the basket and end up getting stuck face first in the basket with his legs flailing out the top. Judge me as you will, but we thought it was so cute we would always take a picture or two, or even a short video, before helping him out of the basket. Although this was extremely entertaining, I now prefer to store toys for babies in a basket they can actually reach into the bottom of without getting stuck. This fabric basket is ideal for little ones because the sides will squish down if leaned on. It's also super flexible and large, making it great for transporting all sorts of baby gear.

FINISHED SIZE
14" diameter at base x 13" tall

SKILL LEVEL

Easy

MATERIALS

Yardage is based on 42"-wide fabric unless otherwise noted.

1¼ yards of quilting cotton for exterior*

1¼ yards of quilting cotton for interior*

1¼ yards of 72"-wide craft felt for stabilizer

16" square of paper or pattern-making material

Decorator fabric, canvas, or duck cloth would also work well.

PATTERN NOTES

◆ The base pattern is on pullout pattern sheet 1.

◆ All seam allowances are ½" and are included in the pattern pieces unless otherwise noted.

◆ Wash, dry, and iron all fabrics before cutting out the pieces.

CUTTING

From the exterior fabric, cut:
2 strips, 3½" x 13½"

From *both* the exterior and interior fabrics, cut:
2 pieces, 14" x 26"
1 base piece

From the craft felt, cut:
4 pieces, 14" x 26"
2 base pieces

2. Baste the Felt to the Fabric

Using the pieces shaped in step 1, baste a felt piece to the wrong side of each interior and exterior fabric piece along all sides of the pieces, about ¼" in from the edges.

3. Sew the Side Pieces

Pin the exterior pieces from step 3 together along the short side edges. Be sure the 24" sides and 26" sides match up with each other, and then stitch the 14" sides together. Press the seam allowances open. Repeat with the interior pieces from step 3.

4. Sew the Base Circles to the Side Pieces

Fold the exterior-fabric base circle in half and pin-mark the fold line at the circle edges. With right sides together, match up the pins to the seam lines of the exterior bin side seams; pin the circle in place. Sew around the circle to attach the base to the bin sides. Repeat with the interior bag side and base circle pieces, but leave an opening of approximately 6" or so through which you can turn the bin to the right side later.

INSTRUCTIONS

Sew all pieces right sides together using a ½" seam allowance unless otherwise noted.

1. Shape the Pieces

Lay an exterior-fabric 14" x 26" piece on your work surface with the long edges at the top and bottom. Make a mark along the bottom edge 1" from each side. Draw a line from the top corners to the marks as shown. Cut along the angled lines. Repeat with the remaining exterior, interior, and felt 14" x 26" pieces.

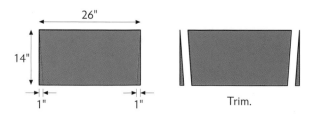

5. Create the Straps

Fold each of the exterior-fabric 3½" x 13½" pieces in half lengthwise, right sides together. Sew along the long, raw edges, ¼" in from the edges. Use a blunt tool, such as a chopstick, to turn each strap right side out. With the seam on the side of the strip, press the straps flat. Topstitch along each long side of the straps, about ⅛" in from the edges.

6. Assemble the Bin

Turn the exterior bin piece right side out. Pin a strap to one side of the bin so the ends are 3" from the side seams. Repeat on the opposite side. Place the exterior bin inside the interior bin, right sides together. Match up the top raw edges and pin them together. Sew around the top of the bin.

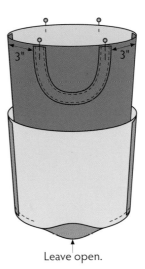

Leave open.

7. Turn the Bin

Turn the bin right side out through the opening at the base of the interior bin. Topstitch the opening closed about ¼" in from the edge.

8. Topstitch the Top Edge

Push the interior bin inside the exterior bin. Pin around the top to flatten the seam. Working about ¼" in from the edge, topstitch around the top edge of the bin. It's helpful to use a heavy-duty needle (size 16 or 18) and stitch very slowly over thick sections, such as across the side seams.

You're done! Grab something that needs organizing or transporting and throw it in your bin.

Karate Pants

I was always buying pants for Presley until I realized how easy they are to make. This simple pattern is designed to fit even cloth-diapered baby bums. Make a dozen pairs, especially in the smaller sizes. You'll be glad you did! These may seem like odd sizes, but I never bought clothes in the every-three-month sizes sold for infants. I would have Presley wear a size until it was too small, and then buy two sizes larger and roll up sleeves and hems so he could wear them longer. I used this idea when sizing these pants, because if you're a new mom, you don't have time to be in the sewing room making pants every couple of months! The smallest size is fairly small because tiny babies are very tiny; the other sizes are generous so you can get as much wear out of each as possible.

FINISHED SIZES
3 months (up to about 17 pounds) ◆ 12 months (up to about 22 pounds) ◆ 18 months (up to about 27 pounds)

SKILL LEVEL

Super Easy

MATERIALS

Yardage is based on 42"-wide cotton fabric; you can also use flannel, jersey, or other fabric.

½ yard of fabric for size 3 months;
⅝ yard for size 12 months;
¾ yard for size 18 months

⅔ yard of ⅜"-wide elastic

2 safety pins

PATTERN NOTES

◆ The pants patterns are on pullout pattern sheet 3.

◆ All seam allowances are ¼" and are included in the pattern pieces unless otherwise noted.

◆ Wash, dry, and iron all fabrics before cutting out the pieces.

CUTTING

From the cotton fabric, cut:
2 pants pieces in your desired size, placing the pattern fold line on the lengthwise fold of fabric

These pants can have any personality you want based on your fabric choice.

INSTRUCTIONS

Sew all pieces right sides together using a ¼" seam allowance unless otherwise noted. Refer to "Seam Finishes" on page 94 for seam-finishing options.

1. Sew the Pants

Align the front and back pants pieces. Sew the inner leg/crotch seam, starting at the bottom of one leg and stitching around the crotch and back down to the bottom of the other leg. Then sew the two outer side seams. Finish seams as desired.

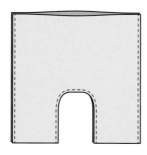

2. Sew the Hems and Casing

Fold up the bottom edge of each leg ¼" to the wrong side; press. Fold up the bottom edge ¼" again; press and pin in place. Stitch along the top folded edge to hem each leg. Fold down the waist edge ¼" to the wrong side; press. Fold down the waist edge ¾"; press and pin in place. Stitch along the bottom folded edge, leaving a 1" opening to insert the elastic.

MEASURING ELASTIC

The best way to measure the elastic for the waist is to measure your child's waist or the waistline of a well-fitting pair of nonelastic pants. However, some general lengths of elastic are 14" for the 3-month size, 16" for the 12-month size, and 18" for the 18-month size. The finished size on each of these will be 1" less when you've sewn the elastic together.

3. Add the Elastic

Cut a piece of elastic to the length needed. Pin a safety pin to each end of the elastic. Pin one end to one side of the waist opening. Use the other pin to slide the elastic through the casing, being careful not to twist it. Carefully unpin the elastic end that you pinned to the waist opening, remove both safety pins, and overlap the ends 1"; securely sew the ends together. Pop the elastic back into the casing and sew the opening closed.

Find a kid who needs some pants. We always call Presley "Peter Pants-less" when he escapes and runs around with no pants on.

Knit Hat

You will love this hat. Of all the things I made for Presley, this and his sheets are probably the two that were used the most. I made a hat like this when he was born by tracing around a commercially made hat for size and shape and then creating my own. We took it to the hospital and he wore it every day for the first few weeks. He even slept in it for several months! Not only do I wish I had made more than one (seriously, the commercially made hats never fit or stayed on like the one I made), but I found myself wishing I had a larger-sized one as well. So, here you go. Take it from me, make several of these in the smallest size, and then make the larger size if you find yourself wanting a hat like this when your wee one gets bigger.

FINISHED SIZES
Newborn: 14" circumference, unstretched ◆ 6 months: 16" circumference, unstretched

SKILL LEVEL

Super Easy

MATERIALS

¼ yard of cotton or cotton-blend jersey or other knit fabric for hat top and cuff

PATTERN NOTES

- The hat patterns are on pullout pattern sheet 3.
- All seam allowances are ¼" and are included in the pattern pieces unless otherwise noted.
- Wash, dry, and iron all fabrics before cutting out the pieces.

CUTTING

Cut pieces for desired size.

Newborn

From the jersey, cut:
2 hat pieces
1 strip, 6" x 14½"

6 Months

From the jersey, cut:
2 hat pieces
1 strip, 7" x 16½"

INSTRUCTIONS

Sew all pieces right sides together using a ¼" seam allowance unless otherwise noted. Refer to "Seam Finishes" on page 94 for seam-finishing options.

1. Create the Cuff

Fold the jersey strip in half crosswise, right sides together, and sew the short ends together to create a loop. With the seam and raw edges aligned, fold the loop in half lengthwise, right sides out, to create the hat cuff.

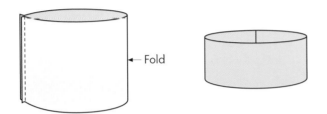

2. Sew the Top of the Hat

Sew the hat pieces together along the curved edge, leaving the long straight edge open.

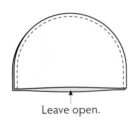

3. Sew the Cuff to the Top of the Hat

With the top of the hat still wrong side out, insert the hat cuff into the hat, aligning the raw edges and matching the cuff seam with one of the hat seams. Pin and then sew the cuff in place. Finish the raw edges as desired. Turn the hat right side out. Fold up the cuff so that it covers the seam. You can tack the cuff in place by sewing a couple of stitches through all the layers on each side. I didn't tack mine, and had no trouble keeping the cuff in place.

Find a teeny-weeny newbie baby and protect its tiny head with this tiny hat.

Though cute in solid colors, these hats are particularly suited for prints.

Baby Leg Warmers

Oh, how I love baby leg warmers. There are so many adorable ones to choose from these days. But they're pricey; even knock-off brands will cost you eight bucks or more a pair—for essentially footless socks. When Presley was first born they were all he wore. We listened to everyone who said, "Don't buy newborn-sized clothes. They grow out of them in two weeks!" So we only bought two pairs of jammies in the newborn size, and Presley swam in them—for months. He's always been fairly small, so he ended up in a Onesie and leg warmers for the first six months because nothing else fit! I wish I'd known then that I could use knee-high socks to make leg warmers, because they're only a dollar or two at big-box stores. I'll spend $2 over $8 any day!

FINISHED SIZE
Depending on the socks you use, these will fit up to a three-year-old or so as leg warmers, then up to 10 years old as arm warmers.

SKILL LEVEL
Super Easy

MATERIALS
1 pair of women's knee-high socks

PATTERN NOTES
- All seam allowances are ¼".
- Wash and dry the socks before cutting them.

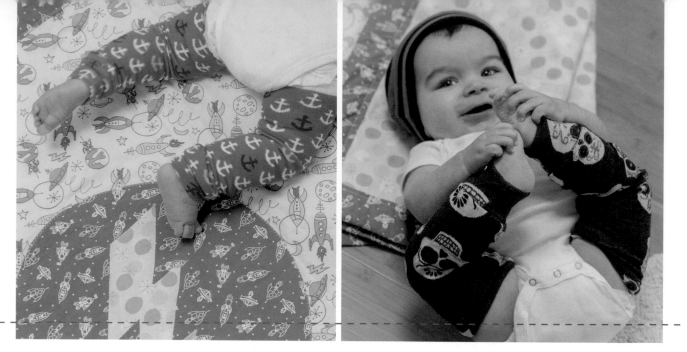

Baby Leg Warmers in alternate colorways

INSTRUCTIONS

Sew all pieces right sides together using a ¼" seam allowance unless otherwise noted. Refer to "Seam Finishes" on page 94 for seam-finishing options.

1. Create the Leg

Cut straight across each sock above the heel through both layers, making sure the socks are the same length.

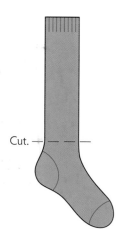

Cut.

2. Create the Bottom Cuff

From one of the heel portions you cut off in step 1, cut a straight line right below the heel and another right above the toe to create a small tube. Turn each tube inside out, flatten the tube, and then sew down the length of the tube, about ¾" from the edge, to make the cuff. Make sure the cuff stretches perpendicular to the seam as shown. The seam will make the cuff narrower than the leg and keep it snug around the ankle and off your baby's foot. Trim the seam allowances to about ¼". Repeat with the remaining heel portion to make a second cuff.

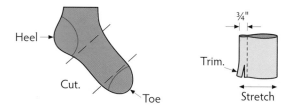

Heel

Cut.

Toe

¾"

Trim.

Stretch

3. Sew the Cuffs to the Legs

Fold each cuff tube in half lengthwise, wrong sides together with the seam aligned. Insert a leg from step 1 into each cuff, right side out and raw edges aligned. Position the cuff seam so it points inward toward the "ankle" part of the leg; pin the raw edges together. Sew the raw edges together, stretching the pieces as needed to fit. Finish the seam allowances as desired.

Find a baby in a Onesie and tuck those cute little legs into some leg warmers!

Wearable Blanket

When Presley was born, we were "rule follower" parents and swaddled him for sleep, nice and tight every night. One morning when he was about three weeks old, I walked in to find him on his face! He'd rolled right over and, thanks to the swaddling, had no arms and no chance whatsoever of rolling back or even moving his face away from the mattress and sheet. We went right out and bought a wearable blanket, and he slept in one every nap and nighttime until he was almost two. These can be pricey, though, because you need multiples so you can wash them regularly. I bought one per size and then made several more. They're so easy to make, I could even sew one when Presley was a newborn and I had exactly zero time to myself. Make a couple of these—you'll use the heck out of them!

FINISHED SIZE
One size fits up to about one year old.
Chest: 11½" wide at armholes, 14½" wide at widest point ◆ Length: 28" long

SKILL LEVEL

 Super Easy

MATERIALS

Yardage is based on 54"-wide fabric.

1 yard of ultra-plush fleece, or a fabric with edges that won't fray

24"-long zipper to coordinate with fabric (see "Pattern Notes," right)

Sharp thread snips or a seam ripper

Transparent tape

PATTERN NOTES

◆ The blanket pattern is on pullout pattern sheet 3.

◆ All seam allowances are ¼" and are included in the pattern piece unless otherwise noted.

◆ Wash, dry, and iron your fabric using the appropriate temperature settings before cutting out the pieces.

◆ You can use a 20"-long zipper if you can't find a 24"-long one. I just like a longer zipper to allow the blanket to open more, making it easier to get off a squirmy baby.

CUTTING

From the ultra-plush fleece, cut:

1 back piece, placing center front/back line on fold of fabric

2 front pieces, reversing 1 (fold the fabric so the right or wrong sides are together and cut around all of the pattern edges to make 2 separate pieces that are mirror images of each other)

SIZE IT UP

Because the pattern piece is so large, I only included one size, which should fit up to about a one-year-old. To make a bigger size, increase an inch or two (or three) along the center edge, as well as another inch or two (or more) in the length. You can extend the neck and arm openings by cutting the neck a little deeper and the arms a little lower.

INSTRUCTIONS

Sew all pieces right sides together using a ¼" seam allowance unless otherwise noted.

1. Finish the Neck and Arm Openings

Fold under the neck- and arm-opening edges on the front and back pieces ¼" to the wrong side. Set your iron on low. Press under, and then pin the folded edges in place; topstitch about ⅛" from the edges.

2. Baste the Zipper in Place

With *wrong* sides together, pin the front pieces together along the center front edges. Be sure you're pinning the long, straight edges and not the edges that have the rounded corner at the bottom. Using the longest stitch length on your machine, baste ¼" from the pinned edges. Do not backstitch this seam; you'll rip it out later. Press the seam allowances open. Working on the wrong side of the fabric, lay the zipper right side down over the center seam, lining up the top edge of the zipper tape with the edge of the neckline and the zipper teeth with the seam. Tape the zipper in place.

3. Stitch the Zipper

Using your zipper foot, begin at the top of one side of the zipper and sew right next to the zipper teeth to just below the metal stop; pivot, sew back and forth across the end of the zipper (just below the metal stop), and then pivot and sew right next to the zipper teeth up to the top. Move the zipper pull out of the way as you come to it. Remove the tape. Turn the piece over to the right side and use a seam ripper to remove the basting along the length of the zipper. Restitch the remainder of the seam below the zipper using a regular stitch length.

4. Assemble the Blanket

Pin the front and back pieces together. Sew across both shoulders, backstitching at each edge. Sew around the sides and bottom of the blanket, beginning at one underarm and sewing around to the opposite underarm. Backstitch underarms for an extra-strong join. Turn right side out.

Super easy, right? Make a few more so you always have one ready, even if the rest are in the wash.

Super Crib Sheet

If the thought of making your own crib sheets seems insane, hear me out. When I was pregnant, the idea seemed a little nuts-oid. But I needed specific colors because I was writing my book Knit a Monster Nursery *(Martingale, 2012). No surprise, I couldn't find a crib sheet that matched the nursery colors. So I bought heavy interlock knit fabrics in bright colors and whipped up a few sets of sheets. To this day the sheets I made are the only ones we use on Presley's bed. They're one of my favorite things I made for him. The pattern allows you to mix two woven cotton fabrics—one on top and a contrasting fabric on the sides. We didn't use a crib skirt, so an extra punch of color on the sides of the mattress is cute and fun! I suggest you make three or four sets of these sheets. You'll be glad you did.*

FINISHED SIZE
Fits a standard 28" x 52" crib mattress that's 5" to 6" deep; check your mattress dimensions and adjust your pieces as necessary.

SKILL LEVEL

Super Easy

MATERIALS

Yardage is based on 42"-wide fabric unless otherwise noted.

1½ yards of quilting cotton for top
1½ yards of nondirectional quilting cotton for sides*
1½ yards of ½"-wide elastic
2 safety pins

If using 54" or wider fabric, you'll need ⅞ yard of a nondirectional print.

PATTERN NOTES

- All seam allowances are ½" and are included in the cutting dimensions.
- Wash, dry, and iron all fabrics before cutting out the pieces.

CUTTING

From the top fabric, cut:
1 piece, 29" x 53"

From the side fabric, cut:*
2 strips, 9½" x 53"
2 strips, 9½" x 29"

With 42"-wide fabric, these pieces will need to be cut from the lengthwise grain rather than the width of the fabric (selvage to selvage). Double-check your fabric; if it has a directional print and you cut the pieces lengthwise, you may not be happy with the results.

INSTRUCTIONS

Sew all pieces right sides together using a ½" seam allowance unless otherwise noted. Refer to "Seam Finishes" on page 94 for seam-finishing options.

1. Sew the Short Sides

Pin and then sew the 9½" x 29" side strips to the short ends of the 29" x 53" sheet top, aligning the raw edges. Press the seam allowances open.

Note: If you're using a directional print for the side fabric, make sure it's oriented the way you want it to look when on the bed. The raw edge at this point will be the bottom of the sheet.

2. Sew the Long Sides

Pin the 9½" x 53" side strips to the long sides of the sheet top, aligning the raw edges. Be sure the end pieces are out of the way of the seam line. Beginning and ending ½" from the ends, sew the strips to the top. Press the seam allowances open.

3. Create the Corners

At one corner, hold the two short ends of the sheet sides right sides together. Pin in place and then sew, starting at the outside edge and sewing toward the sheet top. Repeat for the other three corners. Finish these seams as desired.

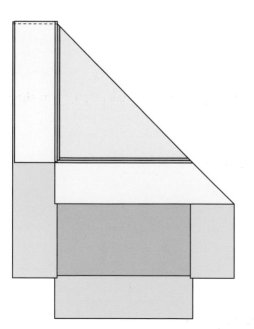

4. Make the Casing

Fold under and press the bottom raw edge ½" to the wrong side of the fabric. After you've gone around the whole sheet, fold under the edge another ¾" and press again, and then pin in place. Topstitch ⅛" from the first folded edge, leaving a 2" to 3" opening between the beginning and end of your seam for inserting the elastic, and backstitch at the beginning and end of the stitching line.

5. Add the Elastic

Pin a safety pin to each end of the elastic. Pin one end to one side of the casing opening. Use the other pin to slide the elastic through the casing, being careful not to twist the elastic. Carefully unpin the elastic end that you pinned to the casing opening, remove both safety pins, and overlap the ends 1"; securely sew the ends together. Pop the elastic back into the casing and sew the opening closed.

Done! Go make a bed. It will be much more fun with a handmade sheet!

● SINGLE-COLOR SHEETS

If you don't want a multicolored sheet, you'll need one piece of fabric, 46" x 70". Fold the piece in half vertically and horizontally, and then cut a 9" x 9" square through all the layers from the corner without any folds. Continue the instructions as written, starting with step 3. I'm particularly fond of knit fabrics (which are available in 54"-widths) for single-color sheets.

Counting Sheep Mobile

In my opinion, no nursery is complete without an outstanding mobile above the crib. I made one for Presley using the pattern from Knit a Monster Nursery, and it's still hanging above his crib, even though he's now sleeping in a toddler bed. We all just adore his mobile. I wanted to make one to sew that was just as cute. I love this mobile! Who doesn't want to fall asleep under cute, fluffy, cloudlike sheep? Make this for your own nursery, or for a friend's, and it's sure to become a cherished item that will be remembered forever.

FINISHED SIZE
14" diameter x 23" from hoop to top of sheep

SKILL LEVEL

Easy

MATERIALS

Yardage is based on 72"-wide fabric, unless otherwise noted.

¼ yard *OR* 4 sheets (9" x 12") of black craft felt

¼ yard *OR* 4 sheets of white craft felt

1 sheet of dark-gray craft felt

1 yard of jumbo pom-pom trim

Hand-sewing needle

Embroidery floss in black, white, and gray

Fabric glue

Gray puffy fabric paint for eyes

14" wooden embroidery hoop (inner hoop only)

Craft paint to match nursery decor for hoop

Foam paintbrush

Approximately 14 yards of fingering-weight yarn in a color to match hoop paint for hanging mobile

1¼"-diameter silver O ring (I used one intended for purse hardware)

Hot-glue gun and glue sticks

5 medium-size binder clips

PATTERN NOTES

◆ Patterns for all sheep pieces are on pullout pattern sheet 2.

CUTTING

From the white felt, cut:
8 body pieces
4 hair pieces

From the black felt, cut:
40 leg pieces
10 ear pieces
5 face pieces

Continued on page 39

Continued from page 37

From the dark-gray felt, cut:
2 body pieces
1 hair piece

From the yarn, cut:
15 pieces, 12" long
15 pieces, 20" long

INSTRUCTIONS

1. Make the Legs

Using the fabric glue, glue two leg pieces together. Repeat to make a total of 20 legs. Using a running stitch (see illustration below) and three strands of black floss, sew ⅛" from the edge around the two long sides and the rounded end of each leg, leaving the straight top edge unstitched. Lining up the top of the legs with the marks on the body pattern, glue four legs to the wrong sides of four white body pieces and one dark-gray body piece.

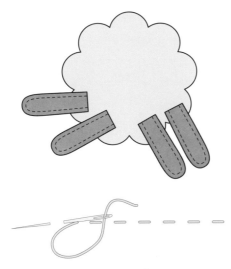

Running stitch

2. Make the Faces

Using the marks on the face pattern piece, glue two ears to the right side of each face piece, with the larger end pointing outward. Then, glue one hair piece to the top of each face, covering the smaller end of each ear. Add two dots of gray puffy fabric paint for the eyes now. Glue the faces to the right sides of the remaining body pieces (without legs) as indicated on the pattern. Let the glue and paint dry. Using the matching color of floss and a running stitch, sew around each hair piece, catching the ears as you go. Using black floss and a running stitch, stitch around the black part of each face, catching the body piece behind the face, and just sewing through the face where it hangs over the edge of the body.

3. Braid the Yarn

Bundle the 12"-long pieces of yarn into five sets of three pieces each. Tie a knot in one end of the pieces and braid each set of yarn; tie a knot at the end of each braided piece. Repeat with the 20"-long pieces of yarn.

4. Sew the Sheep Bodies

Using fabric glue, glue one end of each shorter braid to the center top on the wrong side of the five body pieces with the legs. Using two body pieces of the same color and matching up the bumps, glue each front body piece (face side) to a back body piece (leg side), wrong sides together, sandwiching the legs between the pieces. Once the glue has dried, use a running stitch and a corresponding floss color to sew the two body pieces together around the outer edges, being sure to catch the yarn in your stitching. Start and stop sewing behind the face, lifting the face out of the way as needed.

5. Paint the Hoop

Using the craft paint and the foam brush, paint all sides of the inner embroidery hoop. Once dry, paint the hoop again with a second coat.

6. Attach the Hangers to the Hoop

Use the binder clips to temporarily attach the longer braided hanger pieces to the inside of the hoop, placing the ends at about the center of the hoop width. Try to space the hangers as evenly apart as possible. Once attached, pick the hoop up by the loose ends of the hangers to see if the hoop hangs level. Adjust as necessary and then remove each binder clip and hot glue each hanger to the inside of the hoop. Tie the loose ends of the braids together in a knot.

7. Attach the Sheep to the Hoop

Using the same method as with the hangers, use the binder clips to attach the braided yarn pieces that are attached to each sheep, placing them so they hang below the hoop and are between the hangers. Pick up the hoop again to make sure it hangs straight, then remove the binder clips as you hot glue each of the braids to the inside of the hoop.

8. Attach the Pom-Pom Trim

Hot glue the tape edge of the pom-pom trim to the bottom inside edge of the hoop. You can use the binder clips to test the placement of the trim edge so that the pom-poms hang down to your liking. Overlap the ends an inch or so, and then cut off the excess trim.

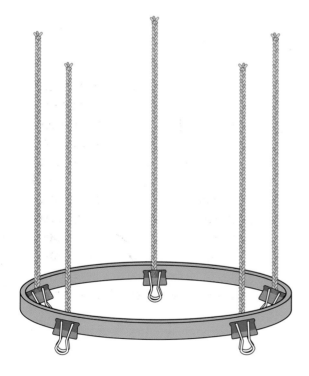

⊛ COUNTING SHEEP

I chose not to, but I think this mobile would be darling with a number added to each of the sheep. You could either cut each number out of felt and embroider it on as you did for the body parts, or use the puffy fabric paint to write each number. Either way, numbers or not, felt or puff paint, this mobile is sure to be the centerpiece of your nursery.

White and dark-gray counting sheep

9. Finish the Mobile

Hold the hanger ends together and tie a loop about 5" from the ends. Put your thumb in the loop to keep it open. Slide the ends through the ring, then tuck them back down through the loop. Tighten the loop to create a knot and secure the ends to the ring. Once the knot is tightened, trim the ends. Put a few dots of hot glue on the trimmed ends to keep the knot from coming out.

All done! Now go find a baby in a crib and hang this up.

YOU SPIN ME ROUND

Obviously, this mobile doesn't spin on its own, which has been fine in our nursery. We simply set up a mini-fan and pointed it at the mobile for a little air flow in the nursery and to get it to spin. If you want yours to spin, either copy our trick or look for a thrift-shop mobile and take it apart so you can reuse the turning mechanism. I've heard you can purchase new mobile spinners, but I've never been able to find one. Whatever you choose, this mobile will be amazing, whether it turns or not.

Baa the Bedtime Buddy

Holy cow, you should see Presley's bedtime routine. We waited a long time before allowing anything in bed with him. Around age two, things changed. It started with a beautiful monster quilt a friend made for him. Then we added his "Super Bear" (see page 11). Next, a purchased stuffed monster. Then I made him a stuffed monster that also had to come to bed. Finally, we added this sheep (which is now his favorite thing to sleep with), plus a bear and another handmade pillow. All seven of these have to be put in bed every nap and nighttime and come out of bed one by one as he names them. What a riot! I hope you share joys like this with your kids.

Baa is filled with a purchased pillow form so that you can remove and wash the cover without worrying about the stuffing becoming lumpy.

FINISHED SIZE
Fits a standard 12"-diameter round pillow form

SKILL LEVEL

Easy

MATERIALS

Yardage is based on 58"-wide knitted fleece fabric, unless otherwise noted.

½ yard of white or gray fleece for body, tail, and hair

¼ yard of black fleece for face, legs, and ears

Scrap of gray fleece or felt for eyes and nose

9"-long zipper to match body color

12"-diameter round pillow form

Stuffing for legs and tail (optional)

PATTERN NOTES

◆ Patterns for all sheep pieces are on pullout pattern sheet 4.

◆ All seam allowances are ¼" and are included in the pattern pieces unless otherwise noted.

◆ Wash, dry, and iron all fabrics using the appropriate temperature settings before cutting out the pieces.

◆ I used a 9"-long zipper because I wanted as short of a zipper on this guy as possible, knowing it was going to be near munchkin faces. A short zipper can make it tough to get the pillow form in and out, so use a longer zipper if you want your pillow to be easier to stuff.

◆ I used fleece because it's super snuggly and super washable. Jersey would be another excellent choice of fabric here.

CUTTING

From the white or gray fleece, cut:

2 body pieces
2 tail pieces
1 hair piece

From the black fleece, cut:

8 leg pieces
4 ear pieces
1 face piece

From the gray fleece or felt, cut:

2 eyes
1 nose

INSTRUCTIONS

Sew all pieces right sides together using a ¼" seam allowance unless otherwise noted.

1. Sew the Legs, Ears, and Tail

Place two leg pieces together and sew around the curved edges, leaving the top, straight edge open. Repeat with the remaining leg pieces and the two tail pieces to make a total of four legs and one tail. In the same manner, sew two ear pieces together, leaving the concave curves open as indicated on the pattern. Repeat to make a total of two ears. Turn each of the pieces right side out. Fold under the open ends of two legs and the tail about ¼" to the wrong side. Press or pin the folded edges in place.

2. Create the Face

Lightly transfer the nose lines from the face pattern to the right side of the face piece. Draw a line from the center bottom of the nose to the edge of the face. Set your sewing machine for a wide-width and short-length zigzag stitch, and thread your machine with gray thread. Stitch on the marked line. It can be helpful to use a piece of paper or stabilizer behind this line to make the stitching smoother. Pin the nose in place so it just covers the end of the stitching line. Pin the eyes in place, referring to

the pattern as necessary. With matching thread, carefully topstitch around each piece about ⅛" from the edge.

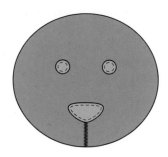

3. Attach the Face, Front Legs, Ears, and Hair

Stuff the legs and tail if desired. (I did not stuff them on the pillow shown.) Place the face right side up and the two legs with the folded top edges on the right side of the body front where indicated on the pattern; pin in place. Fold the ears in half lengthwise, matching the curved edges along the open end. Slip the open end of the ears under the sides of the face and pin in place. Topstitch around the face, catching the ears as you go. Topstitch along the folded edge of each leg, stitching over the seam line two or three times and backstitching at the beginning and end to secure the legs to the body. With right sides up, place the hair on top of the face where indicated on the pattern and topstitch about ⅛" from the edges.

4. Baste the Back Legs in Place

Place the remaining two legs on the right side of the body front where indicated on the pattern, aligning the raw edges; pin in place. Baste the legs in place ⅛" from the edges.

Baste.   Baste.

5. Sew on the Tail

Pin the tail to the right side of the back body piece where indicated on the pattern. Topstitch along the folded edge of the tail, stitching over the seam line two or three times and backstitching at the beginning and end to secure the tail to the body.

6. Put in the Zipper

Refer to "Putting in a Zipper" (page 89) to stitch the zipper in place on the bottom of the body pieces.

7. Sew around the Body

Matching up the bumps and aligning the zipper ends, pin the front and back body pieces together. Open the zipper halfway. Beginning at one end of the zipper, sew around the body to the other end of the zipper. Be sure you're catching the zipper tape above the top stop and below the bottom stop so the seam will be completely closed when the zipper is zipped.

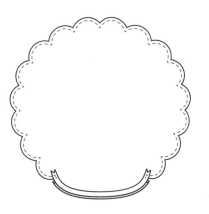

8. Topstitch the Bumps

Turn the body right side out, checking that all of the bumps turn out completely. With your iron on the appropriate setting for your fabric, press all the bumps flat. To make the bumps stand out more once the pillow insert is in place, topstitch about ⅛" from the edge of the body along all the bumps.

Insert the pillow form and go start a new bedtime routine with a little person!

Baa has lots of limbs and even a tail on the back for little hands to explore.

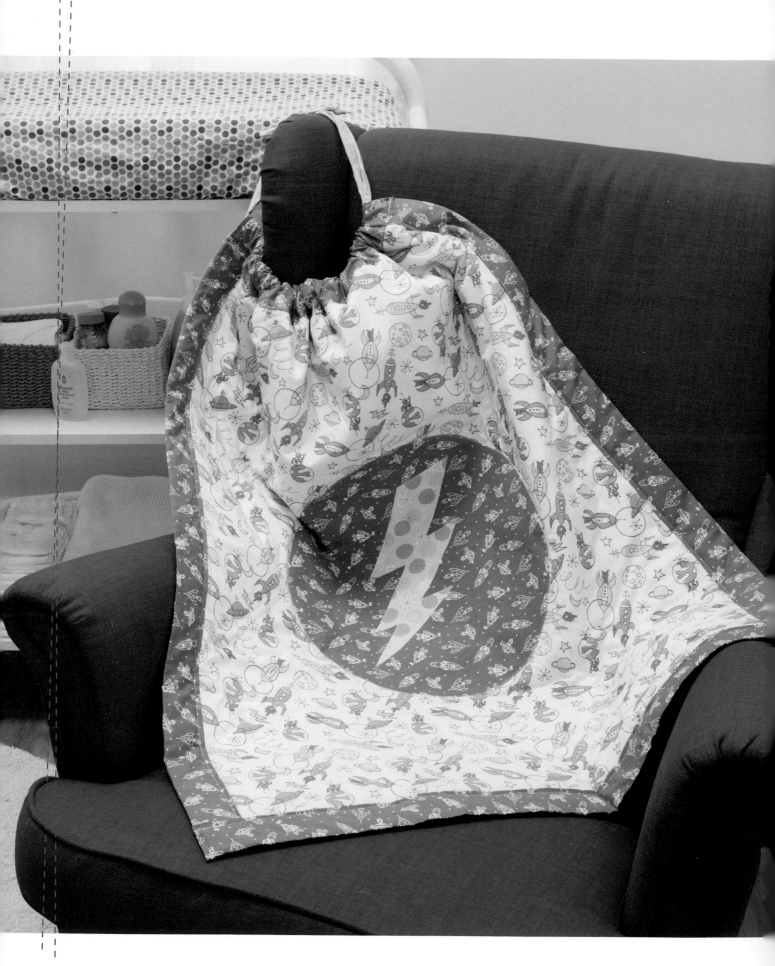

Superhero Blanket

Presley became really interested in capes and superheroes just after his second birthday. He'd request capes all the time, so I'd tie a blanket around his neck and watch him take off running all over our house. This got me to thinking, "How cool would it be to have a blanket that somehow turned into a cape?" After a ton of thought, I came up with this—a cape with drawstring ties that disappear when you want a blanket! I have to say I'm pretty pleased with the result, and Presley loves his. And who doesn't want a blanket with a superhero emblem on it? Make this for the next baby shower you attend, and it's sure to be the hit present!

FINISHED SIZE
30" x 36"

SKILL LEVEL

 Easy

MATERIALS

Yardage is based on 42"-wide fabric.

1⅛ yards of cotton or flannel for circle appliqué and binding

1⅛ yards of cotton or flannel for tie, blanket back, and lightning-bolt appliqué

1 yard of cotton or flannel for blanket front

30" x 36" piece of low-loft batting (I used Pellon Legacy rayon batting)

½ yard of 18"-wide paper-backed fusible web

Safety pin

Walking foot (optional)

PATTERN NOTES

- The circle and lightning-bolt appliqué patterns are on pullout pattern sheet 1.

- All seam allowances are ¼" and are included in the pattern pieces unless otherwise noted.

- Wash, dry, and iron all fabrics before cutting out the pieces.

- I recommend using an open-toe or appliqué foot for sewing the appliqués in place, and a walking foot for all other sewing. Though not required, a walking foot will make it much easier to keep the layers from shifting as you sew them together.

CUTTING

From the blanket-front fabric, cut:
1 rectangle, 30" x 36"

From the blanket-back fabric, cut:
1 rectangle, 30" x 36"
1 strip, 3½" x 36"

From the fabric for binding, cut:
4 strips, 5" x 42"

INSTRUCTIONS

Sew all pieces right sides together using a ¼" seam allowance unless otherwise noted.

1. Prepare the Appliqués

Trace the circle and lightning-bolt patterns onto the paper side of the fusible web. Roughly cut out each shape. Follow the manufacturer's instructions to fuse the fusible-web pieces to the wrong sides of the appropriate fabrics. Cut out each shape on the marked lines. Do not remove the paper backing yet.

2. Appliqué the Design

Pin the batting rectangle to the wrong side of the blanket-front rectangle and baste it in place, sewing about ¼" from all of the edges. Remove the paper backing from the lightning-bolt shape. Visually center it on the fabric circle and fuse it in place. Remove the paper backing from the circle shape. Fold the blanket front and the circle appliqué in half vertically and horizontally and crease the folds to mark the centers. With right sides up and the centers matching, fuse the circle to the center of the blanket front. Using a medium-length, medium- to narrow-width zigzag stitch, sew around the edge of the circle, catching the circle fabric with the zig and the blanket fabric with the zag. Stitch the lightning bolt in place in the same manner.

3. Baste the Blanket Back and Front Together

Turn the blanket front over so the batting is facing up. Lay the back piece over the batting, right side up. Baste the backing to the front/batting piece, sewing about ¼" from all of the edges.

4. Create the Binding Strips

Fold under the long edges of each 5" x 42" binding strip ½" to the wrong side. Fold under one short end of each binding strip to the wrong side ½" and press in place. Press the strip in half, wrong sides together.

⊙ SAFETY FIRST!

Infant and toddler safety is of utmost importance. Though the ties on this blanket store on the inside of the blanket, please use discretion when letting an infant or toddler sleep with this item. If you think that your child might be able to get the tie out of the blanket and cause a hazard in bed, reserve the blanket for use in a stroller or in other settings that will involve adult supervision.

5. Bind the Sides

Sandwich one long side of the blanket between a binding strip, butting the edge of the blanket up to the center fold of the binding. Align the folded end with the top edge of the blanket. Pin the binding in place, starting at the top edge and stopping just a few inches from the bottom corner. Trim the end of the binding ½" past the bottom of the blanket, and then fold under the end ½" so it's aligned with the blanket bottom edge. Stitch the binding in place ⅛" from the edge of the binding. Repeat on the opposite long side of the blanket.

6. Bind the Bottom

Sandwich the bottom edge of the blanket between one of the remaining binding strips in the same manner as you did on the sides, trimming and folding under the raw end so it is flush with the side. Starting at the bottom-left corner of the bottom binding with a backstitch, stitch across the binding end, stopping ⅛" from the top of the binding. Pivot, and then stitch across the top of the bottom binding, stopping ⅛" from the end; pivot and stitch to the bottom-right corner; backstitch.

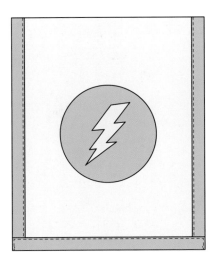

7. Attach the Tie Casing

Sandwich the top edge of the blanket between the remaining binding strip in the same manner as you did on the bottom, trimming and folding under the raw end so it's flush with the side. Remove the binding strip and open it up. Topstitch ⅛" from the short, folded ends. Pin the binding to the top of the blanket as you've done with the other three edges. Topstitch ⅛" from the long folded-under edges. You want the ends to be open to slide in the tie, so don't sew around the corners like you did on the bottom.

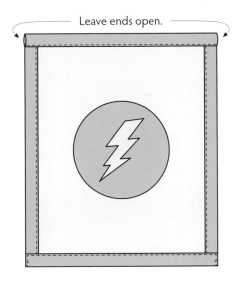

Leave ends open.

8. Create the Tie

Fold under the short ends of the 3½" x 36" tie strip ½" to the wrong side and press in place. Fold the strip in half lengthwise, right sides together. Stitch along the long raw edges. Press the seam allowances open. Turn the strip right side out and press. Topstitch around the entire strip, about ⅛" from the edges.

9. Attach the Tie

Tie a knot in one end of the tie, right at the end. Attach a safety pin to the other end and use it to slide the tie through the casing. Once the tie is through to the other side, tie a knot in this end as well. Be sure that the knotted ends line up right with the sides of the casing. With the tie spaced evenly on each end, fold the top edge of the blanket in half lengthwise to determine the center. Mark the center with a pin, and then sew down the center of the binding to hold the tie in place.

Now find a kid who needs a superhero cape. That shouldn't be too hard to do—even Mr. Danger tried to steal this sample!

Mei Tai Baby Carrier

Baby carriers can be pricey, and since we wanted to try several kinds, I bought a pattern and made a mei tai similar to this one. It was by far the most-used baby item when Presley was an infant. He literally spent 90% of the day in this until he was about three months old. The first few weeks, the only way we could get him to sleep at night would be to bundle him up in it and sleep on the couch, propped up with him on Mom's or Dad's chest.

I often wished my mei tai had been a little different, so I've made several improvements with this version. I added a hood so the baby's little head can't flop out the side, and some padding to make it more comfortable for everyone. Even if you're not sure about wearing a baby, you should give this carrier a try. I really can't say enough good things about it.

FINISHED SIZE
Fits babies from 12 to 35 pounds

SKILL LEVEL

Intermediate

MATERIALS

Yardage is based on 54"-wide fabric unless otherwise noted.

2⅝ yards of bottom-weight fabric like canvas, twill, or duck cloth for pocket and back of body, hood, and straps

¾ yard of 42"-wide quilting-weight print for front of body, hood, and straps

⅝ yard of heavy-duty canvas for lining

35" x 35" square of batting for body and strap padding (pick the batting weight depending on how warm you want your carrier to be)

2 rubber bands

PATTERN NOTES

◆ The body and hood patterns are on pullout pattern sheet 4.

◆ All seam allowances are ½" and are included in the pattern pieces unless otherwise noted.

◆ Wash, dry, and iron all fabrics before cutting out the pieces.

◆ *Be sure to use a heavy-duty fabric for your carrier.* This will be holding the weight of a baby; you *don't* want something that will rip. Canvas, twill, or duck cloth are the best choices. For more information, see "Canvas and Heavyweight Fabrics" on page 84.

CUTTING

From the bottom-weight fabric, cut:
3 strips, 9" x 84", from the *lengthwise* grain
1 body piece
1 hood piece
1 rectangle, 9" x 19"

From the heavy-duty canvas, cut:
1 body piece
1 square, 19" x 19"

From the quilting-weight print, cut:
1 body piece
1 hood piece
2 strips, 2" x 14"
2 rectangles, 2" x 4"

From the batting, cut:
1 body piece*
2 strips, 12" x 20"
1 rectangle, 12" x 18"

If you live in a particularly warm climate where you're concerned about your baby overheating, you can skip the batting in the body.

INSTRUCTIONS

Sew all pieces right sides together using a ½" seam allowance unless otherwise noted.

1. Make the Shoulder and Waist Straps

Press each bottom-weight 9" x 84" strip in half lengthwise, wrong sides together. Unfold each strip, fold the long edges ½" to the wrong side, and press in place. If you'd prefer angled ends on your straps, refold the strips in half again, cut one end of two of the strips at a 45° angle for the shoulder straps, and cut both ends of the remaining strip at a 45° angle for the waist strap. Open up the strips and press these new raw ends under ½" as well, making a clip a scant ½" at the V to allow both sides to fold under. Set the waist strap aside for later.

2. Add Batting to the Shoulder Straps

Fold each batting 12" x 20" strip in half to create a 6" x 20" rectangle and crease the fold. Unfold the batting and fold each long edge in to meet the center fold line, and then refold the piece in half to create a 3" x 20" piece with the raw edges sandwiched in the center. Unfold the shoulder-strap pieces and lay them wrong side up on your work surface. Place the center fold of a batting piece against the center fold of each strap piece, 5" from the straight end of each strap. Fold each strap in half again along the center fold line and pin the long edges in place. On each strap, topstitch about ⅛" from the long open edges; then, without removing your needle or cutting your thread, pivot and topstitch across the short (angled) end and along the long folded edge as well, leaving one short end open. Working on the padded part, stitch lengthwise through the center of the strap, then 1" in from each edge to hold the padding in place. Finally, sew horizontally across the strap at the top and bottom of the stitching on the padded area.

3. Attach the Loops

Press under the short ends of a quilting-print 2" x 4" rectangle ¼" to the wrong side. Fold the rectangle in half lengthwise, right sides together, and stitch along the long edges. Turn the rectangle to the right side. Press the rectangle, centering the seam. With the seam side facing the shoulder strap, center the rectangle on the padded part of the shoulder strap, 6" from the straight end. Topstitch ⅛" from the pressed-under edges of each rectangle, leaving the long edges open. This will be the right side of the strap.

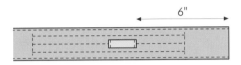

4. Make the Hood

Fold one short end and both long edges of each quilting-print 2" x 14" strip ¼" to the wrong side. Fold each strip in half lengthwise, wrong sides together. Topstitch ⅛" from the folded-under end and long open side. Align the raw end of each strip along the top edge of the bottom-weight hood piece, ¾" from each corner; baste in place. Pin the quilting-print hood piece over the bottom-weight hood piece, sandwiching the ties between the layers. Sew the pieces together along the side and top edges, leaving the bottom straight edge open. Turn the hood right side out and topstitch ⅛" from the finished edges.

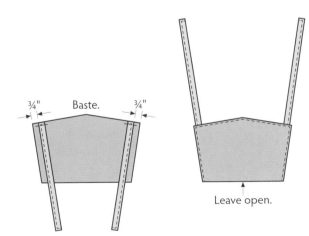

The hood is great for protecting baby from rain or sun.

5. Attach the Straps

Press the strap corners of the heavy-duty canvas body piece ½" to the wrong side. Center and pin a shoulder strap, right side up, to each corner so that the stitching lines of the padded area begin about 1" inside the body piece. Once pinned in place, it's helpful to roll up the straps and secure each one with a rubber band to keep them out of the way while you finish up the mei tai. Stitch a box with an "X" in it above the padded area to secure each strap to the canvas piece. Trim the excess strap even with the folded edge of the shoulder-strap corner.

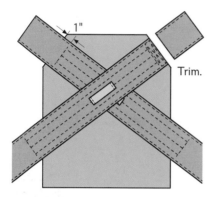

6. Make the Pocket

Refer to "Patch Pockets" (page 93) to make the pocket from the bottom-weight 9" x 19" rectangle.

7. Prepare the Body Pieces

Press the shoulder-strap corners of the quilting-print and bottom-weight body pieces ½" to the wrong side. With right sides facing up, pin the quilting-print body to the heavy-duty canvas body; baste ¼" from the edges, skipping over the shoulder-strap corners. Center the pocket on the right side of the quilting-print body, 6" up from the bottom. Be sure the pocket folded edge is the top edge. Stitch the pocket in place, referring to "Patch Pockets." With the quilting print facing up, pin the hood to the top edge of the body between the straps; baste it in place ¼" from the edges. With the right side facing up, pin the batting body piece

to the wrong side of the bottom-weight body piece. Baste the pieces together, again skipping over the shoulder-strap corners.

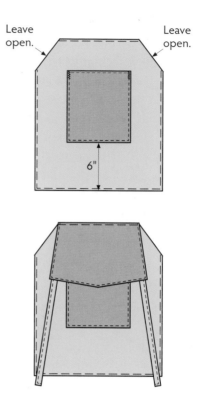

8. Assemble the Body

With right sides together, pin the bottom-weight/ batting piece to the quilting-print/canvas side. Sew the sides together. Sew across the top of the body, not including the shoulders, being careful not to catch the straps in the stitching. Press the seam allowances open. Turn the piece right side out through the open bottom edge. Pull the straps through the corner openings; tuck the seam allowances back in if they come out. Pin the seam allowances on the side, top, and shoulder edges in place and trim away any exposed batting. Topstitch around the side, shoulder-corner, and top edges about ¼" from the edges.

9. Attach the Waist Strap

Pin-mark the center of the bottom edge of the body. Fold the batting 12" x 18" rectangle like you did the shoulder-strap padding in step 2 to make a 3" x 18" piece. With the quilting-print side facing up, center and sandwich the bottom edge of the body between the batting. You'll have about 1" of excess batting extending beyond each side. Find the center of the waist strap by folding it in half widthwise. With the centers matching, sandwich the body and batting between the waist strap; pin it in place, making sure the strap edges are aligned along the full length of the straps. Topstitch along the strap edges and in the padded area, just like you did on the shoulder straps.

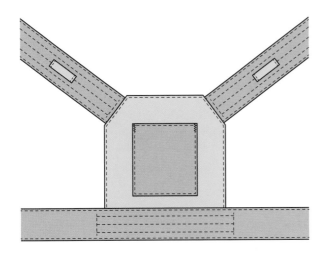

That's it! You're officially prepared to wear a baby. Personally, when I was done making this, I tried it with a stuffed animal because we didn't have a baby at home yet.

WRAP, TIE, AND GO!

With the body piece in front of you (pocket facing outward), wrap the waist straps of the mei tai around your waist and knot them in front. (If they're not long enough, simply knot them in the back.)

Fold the carrier up and place the shoulder straps up and over your shoulders loosely enough so that the baby can fit in the pouch formed by the front flap. Cross the straps in the back, and then bring them to the front. Cross them again at your waist so that the cross will sit under your baby's bottom. If the straps are long enough, wrap them around your waist to the back and tie them in a knot. Otherwise, you can tie them in the front under the pouch. Place the baby in the carrier and off you go!

To use the hood to keep rain or sunshine out of baby's eyes, thread the narrow hood straps through the loops on your shoulder straps and tie in place.

Practice putting on the mei tai once or twice, and then you'll be all set and won't have to refer to the instructions again. Promise!

Diapers-a-Go-Go

Although I once ran a handmade-handbag business, I never wanted to design a full diaper bag for Presley because there are so many awesome ready-made ones. What I did want was a little diaper-change-only bag for quick trips, and this is what I came up with. It's wide enough to fit a stack of large-size diapers on one side and a full package of wipes and a matching changing mat on the other side. It zips up, folds shut, has a strap, and is perfect for changing on the go. You could even drop this into your larger diaper bag, or make two and leave one in the car or stroller so you always have diapers. The matching changing mat fits perfectly with just two folds, so there's no road-map-type refolding. This clutch is even cute enough to use as a fun little bag for you!

FINISHED SIZE
11" x 18", with 18" strap

SKILL LEVEL

Intermediate

MATERIALS

Yardage is based on 42"-wide fabric unless otherwise noted.

⅞ yard of quilting-cotton print for bag lining and changing mat

½ yard of coordinating quilting-cotton print for outer bag

½ yard of polyester/polyurethane laminate (PUL) or other waterproof material for changing mat

1⅝ yards of 20"-wide medium-weight fusible interfacing

2 zippers, 14" long, to coordinate with outer bag fabric

Magnetic purse snap, any size

2 squares, 1" x 1", of felt for snap reinforcement

PATTERN NOTES

♦ All seam allowances are ¼" and are included in the cutting dimensions.

♦ Wash, dry, and iron all fabrics before cutting out the pieces.

♦ I didn't add batting to the changing mat, so it's super flat and doesn't take up much room in the clutch. If you want, you can add a layer of batting or felt to pad it.

CUTTING

From the outer-bag fabric, cut:
1 strip, 11½" x 42"; crosscut into:
    1 rectangle, 11½" x 18½"
    2 rectangles, 7½" x 11½"
    1 rectangle, 4" x 11½"
1 strip, 3½" x 42"; crosscut into:
    1 strip, 3½" x 19"
    1 rectangle, 3½" x 5"

From the bag-lining and changing-mat fabric, cut:
1 strip, 11½" x 42"; crosscut into:
    2 rectangles, 7½" x 11½"
    2 rectangles, 7¾" x 11½"
1 rectangle, 13½" x 21½"

From the laminated fabric, cut:
1 rectangle, 13½" x 21½"

From the interfacing, cut:
1 rectangle, 13½" x 21½"
1 rectangle, 11½" x 18½"
2 rectangles, 7½" x 11½"
1 rectangle, 4" x 11½"
1 strip, 3½" x 19"
1 rectangle, 3½" x 5"

INSTRUCTIONS

Sew all pieces right sides together using a ¼" seam allowance unless otherwise noted.

1. Apply the Interfacing

Follow the manufacturer's instructions to fuse all of the interfacing pieces to the wrong side of the corresponding outer-bag pieces and the laminated fabric rectangle.

Diapers-a-Go-Go bag (top)
and changing mat (bottom)

2. Put in the Zippers

Baste an outer-fabric 7½" x 11½" rectangle to the right side of one half of a zipper so that the zipper pull is ¼" inside the edge of the fabric. (The zipper may extend beyond the other end of the rectangle.) With right sides together, baste a lining 7½" x 11½" rectangle to the wrong side of the same half of the zipper. Fold both rectangles back so they are wrong sides together and topstitch along the edge of the zipper. Place a lining 7¾" x 11½" rectangle behind this piece, right side up, aligning the long edge with the right edge of the zipper; baste in place. Repeat to make two pocket units. Trim off excess zipper tape.

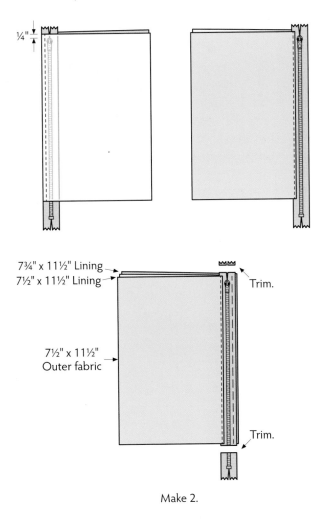

Make 2.

3. Join the Pocket Units

Place the outer-fabric 4" x 11½" rectangle on one pocket unit, aligning the long edge with the right edge of the zipper, right sides together; baste in place. Fold the rectangle back so the right side is up and topstitch along the edge of the zipper. Place the remaining pocket, right sides together, with the zipper edge aligned with the raw edge of the 4" x 11½" rectangle; baste and topstitch in place as before.

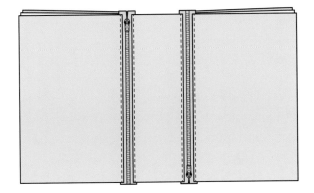

4. Sew the Strap

Fold the outer-fabric 3½" x 19" strip in half lengthwise, right sides together, and sew the long edges together. Press the seam allowances open. Turn the strap right side out. I use a chopstick to make this easier. Press the strap flat, and then topstitch ⅛" in from both long edges. Fold the long sides of the outer-fabric 11½" x 18½" rectangle in half and finger-press a crease at each edge to mark the center. Center and pin the ends of the strap to the piece at these marks, aligning the raw edges; baste ⅛" from the edges.

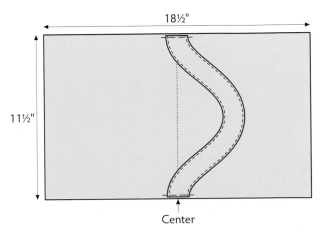

5. Make the Tab Closure

Fold the outer-fabric 3½" x 5" rectangle in half lengthwise, right sides together, to make a 1¾" x 5" piece. Sew the long edges together, leaving both ends open. Measure ½" in from one end of the tab and center a felt square on the wrong side of the tab. Center the flat side of the snap backing on the felt and use a pencil to mark the two rectangular hole positions. Then, making sure you're going through just the felt and one side of the tab, push the sharp tip of a pair of thread nips or a tailor's awl through the felt and one layer of fabric at the marks, creating small holes.

Insert the male portion of the snap through the open end of the tab, and push the snap prongs through the holes. Place the snap back over the prongs and fold the prongs inward. (The prongs can also be folded outward, but if you choose to do this, be careful you don't hit them with the needle when you're topstitching later.) Once the snap is attached, sew across the end of the tab closest to the snap. Turn the tab right side out and press the seams flat. Topstitch around the tab, ⅛" in from the edges.

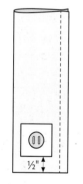 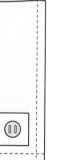 

6. Attach the Tab and Snap to the Outer Bag

Center the tab on the shorter side of the outer-fabric 11½" x 18½" rectangle with the magnet side facing up and raw edges aligned; pin and then baste ⅛" from the raw edges. Measure 1½" in from the opposite end of the piece and center the remaining felt square. Attach the female portion of the snap to the piece in the same manner as for the tab snap.

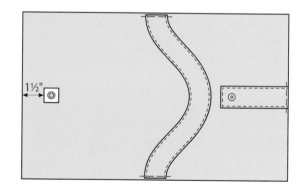

7. Sew the Bag

Open the zippers on the pockets halfway. Align the edges of the strap/tab outer-bag piece with the pocket piece, making sure the tab and strap are sandwiched between the layers. Generously pin the layers together. Starting about 3" from the non-tab side bottom edge, sew toward the corner, pivot, and continue around all of the other sides of the bag. When you get back to the end you started on, pivot and sew about 3" of the side, leaving about 5" or so open in the center. Backstitch at the beginning and end of this seam.

8. Box the Corners

Grab a corner and flatten it out so the center and bottom seams are aligned with each other. Double-check that you have the two lining layers and the pocket layer on one side and just the outer bag on the other. Pin the layers in place. Draw a line 1" from the point of the corner. Sew across the marked line, stitching across it again if you wish. Trim the point, leaving a ¼" seam allowance. Repeat on the remaining three corners of the bag.

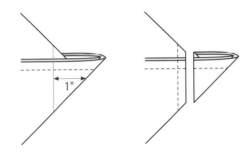

9. Finish the Bag

Turn the bag right side through the opening you left along the bottom edge. Once turned, use a needle and thread that matches your bag and a ladder stitch (page 94) to close the outside layers. Then, with thread that matches the lining, do the same thing on the inside of the pocket.

10. Make the Changing Mat

Pin the changing-mat cotton and laminated-fabric 13½" x 21½" rectangles together. Sew around all four sides, leaving a 4" to 5" opening on one side. Turn the piece right side out. With your iron on a low setting, press on the cotton side of the mat to flatten the seams and fold in the seam allowances along the opening. Topstitch ⅛" from all of the mat edges, closing the opening as you go.

Done! Fold up the changing mat, grab your other diaper supplies, slip everything in the pockets, and go out on an adventure!

Diapers-a-Go-Go in alternate colorway

Pocket Blanket

My book Knit a Monster Nursery is about all the things I knit for Presley's nursery when he was born. One of my favorite projects was a blanket with patch pockets, so when I thought about the projects for this book, a pocket blanket was first on the list. It's so incredibly handy for a baby or toddler! Use it on the floor with toys in the pockets to encourage baby to crawl. Tuck it into the stroller with snacks in the pockets for easy access on a walk. Send it to day care for nap time with a play pal in a pocket. Store wipes in the pockets, use the blanket as a mat, and you have the essentials for a diaper change! This thing is so handy, I wonder why finding a commercially made blanket with pockets is nearly impossible. Make this up in fabrics that match your nursery. You'll love it!

FINISHED SIZE
32" x 48"

SKILL LEVEL

Easy

MATERIALS

Yardage is based on 42"-wide fabric.
Fat quarters are approximately 18" x 21".

1½ yards of quilting cotton for front of blanket

1½ yards of quilting cotton for back of blanket

4 fat quarters of assorted prints for pockets

32" x 48" piece of low-loft batting (I used Pellon Legacy rayon batting)

1 package (4¾ yards) of 2"-wide single-fold satin blanket binding

Walking foot (optional)

PATTERN NOTES

* All seam allowances are ¼" and are included in the cutting dimensions.

* Wash, dry, and iron all fabrics before cutting out the pieces.

* Though not required, a walking foot will make it much easier to keep the layers from shifting as you sew them together.

CUTTING

From *both* the front and back fabrics, cut:
1 rectangle, 32" x 48"

From *each* of the 4 fat quarters, cut:
1 rectangle, 8½" x 18½"

INSTRUCTIONS

Sew all pieces right sides together using a ¼" seam allowance unless otherwise noted.

1. Baste the Front of the Blanket to the Batting

Lay the blanket-front rectangle on the batting, right side up. Baste the pieces together, about ¼" from all of the edges.

2. Make and Attach the Pockets

Refer to "Patch Pockets" (page 93) to make the pockets from the fat-quarter rectangles. Position the top edge of two pockets 9" down from the top edge of the blanket-front piece and 5" in from the sides; pin in place. Position the bottom edge of the remaining two pockets 9" up from the bottom edge of the blanket front and 5" in from the sides; pin in place. Refer to "Patch Pockets" to stitch the pockets in place.

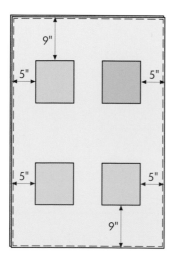

3. Baste the Blanket Back to the Front

Lay the blanket back wrong side up on your work surface. Layer the blanket front over the back, aligning the edges; pin the layers together. Baste the layers together, about ¼" from all of the edges.

4. Sew on the Binding

Refer to "Topstitched Double-Fold Binding" (page 91) to bind the blanket edges, topstitching about ⅛" from the inside edge of the binding. Because these corners are so wide, once you've sewn around all four sides of the blanket, go back and topstitch each corner seam as well. Be sure to backstitch all of your seams.

Tah-dah! All done. Now tuck some snacks and toys into the pockets and go for a walk with a munchkin!

⊙ PIECED BACK

Instead of using a single piece of fabric for the blanket back, you can cut strips from multiple fabrics. Just divide the 48" length of the blanket by the number of fabrics you're using, and add a ½" seam allowance to each piece. For example, if you have six fabrics, cut an 8½"-wide strip of each. Sew them together and use this pieced section as the back of the blanket!

Super Changing-Mat Cover

Diapers are not my favorite thing in the world. Not even close. And those boring, scratchy plastic changing mats at the baby store do not help. Sure they sell covers, but I decided to make my own because I didn't want a Minky-dot changing mat in sky blue (which was all I could find). I'm so glad I did! First, this is just about the simplest project in the whole world. And, I matched mine to my sheets, another win. Each cover takes only 1½ yards of fabric plus elastic, so it's also an inexpensive project. Plus, the ones I made washed so well that they still looked brand-new until Presley was out of diapers. All positive things in my book. I made two and always wished I had made three or four. This is such a quick project, you could probably finish three in one nap time!

FINISHED SIZE
Fits a standard 16" x 32" changing mat that is 3" to 4" deep. Check your changing-mat dimensions and adjust your piece as necessary.

SKILL LEVEL

Super Easy

MATERIALS

1½ yards of quilting cotton or jersey (42" or wider)

1 yard of ⅜"- or ½"-wide elastic

2 safety pins

PATTERN NOTES

◆ All seam allowances are ½" and are included in the cutting dimensions.

◆ Wash, dry, and iron all fabrics before cutting out the pieces.

CUTTING

From the quilting cotton or jersey, cut:
1 rectangle, 32" x 48"

INSTRUCTIONS

Sew all pieces right sides together using a ½" seam allowance unless otherwise noted. Refer to "Seam Finishes" on page 94 for seam-finishing options.

1. Create the Corners

Fold the fabric rectangle in half vertically and horizontally, and then cut an 8" x 8" square through all the layers from the corner without any folds. Open up the piece. At one corner, align the inside edges; pin in place and then sew, starting at the inside corner and sewing toward the outer edge. Repeat on the remaining three corners. Finish the seams as desired.

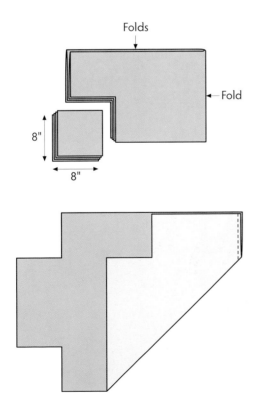

2. Make the Casing

Fold and press under the raw edges ½" to the wrong side of the rectangle. Fold under another ¾" to the wrong side and press again, and then pin the casing in place. (See "Line It Up" on page 89 for an easy way to measure these folds.) Topstitch ⅛" from the first folded edge, leaving a 2" to 3" opening between the beginning and end of your seam to insert the elastic, and backstitching at the beginning and end of the stitching line.

3. Add the Elastic

Attach a safety pin to each end of the elastic. Pin one end to one side of the casing opening. Use the other pin to slide the elastic through the casing, being careful not to twist the elastic. Carefully unpin the elastic end that you pinned to the opening, remove both safety pins, and overlap the ends 1"; securely sew the ends together. Pop the elastic back into the casing and sew the opening closed.

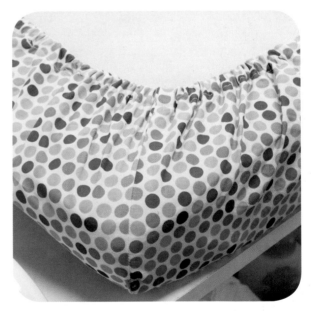

Underside of Super Changing-Mat Cover

There you go—the best changing-mat cover you'll ever use. Now go make a couple more. I promise, you'll want to keep several of these on hand so you always have a clean one when the rest are in the laundry.

Changing Organizer

Holy cupcakes, I wish I'd had one of these for Presley! Our changing area was a mess. We piled everything, diapers and all, into a bin. I was always digging through it one-handed, looking for this or that and becoming irritated. I wanted to get all those supplies up and out of the way. One day I saw a cute little book holder someone had made for a friend's daughter's crib. When her three-year-old woke up she had something to do to encourage her to stay in bed longer. Genius! I got to thinking about my organizer and eureka! A double-duty baby item (we mamas love those, don't we?). This hangs from a dowel on the wall above the changing mat. Once it's safe for baby to have things in the crib, it can hang there. In the future, it can hang from the bed frame for books. You'll use this for years to come!

FINISHED SIZE
12½" x 40½"

SKILL LEVEL

Super Easy

MATERIALS

Yardage is based on 42"-wide cotton fabric.

⅞ yard of print or solid for organizer body

⅝ yard of coordinating print or solid for pocket

26" x 41" piece of batting

5 yards of ⅞"-wide (or wider) ribbon

Point turner

Seam sealant

40" length of ½"-diameter (or larger) dowel if hanging organizer on wall

Craft paint for dowel

Foam paintbrush

Walking foot (optional)

PATTERN NOTES

♦ All seam allowances are ¼" and are included in the cutting dimensions.

♦ Wash, dry, and iron all fabrics before cutting out the pieces.

♦ Though not required, sewing with a walking foot when indicated in the instructions will make it much easier to keep the layers from shifting as you sew them together.

CUTTING

From the body fabric, cut:
2 strips, 13" x 41"

From the pocket fabric, cut:
2 strips, 8½" x 41"

From the batting, cut:
1 piece, 13" x 41"

From the ribbon, cut:
5 pieces, 36" long

⊕ HANGING

The length of the ties doesn't really matter for hanging on the wall, but you'll want to make sure they're long enough to tie around the rail on your crib. My crib has a fairly wide rail, and for the first one of these I made for Presley, I used 24"-long ties which weren't nearly long enough. For the pattern, I decided to make the ties 36" long instead. Depending on what type of crib you have, you might be able to use shorter ties. Measure the ties on your crib to decide, remembering to account for a knot (and for the ribbons being folded in half). You can also make your ties from the pocket fabric. See page 92 for how to make ties from double-fold bias tape.

INSTRUCTIONS

Sew all pieces right sides together using a ¼" seam allowance unless otherwise specified.

1. Assemble the Pocket

Place the pocket strips together, aligning the edges. Stitch across one long edge of the strip. Press the seam allowances open. Fold the piece in half along the seam line so that the wrong sides are together. Topstitch ¼" from the sewn seam.

2. Baste the Batting to the Body

Lay a body-fabric strip, right side up, over the batting piece; pin it in place. If you're using a walking foot, put it on your machine now. You'll be using it for the remainder of the project. Baste the pieces together, ⅛" from all of the edges.

3. Attach the Pocket to the Body

With right sides facing up, lay the pocket on the body piece, aligning the raw edges along the bottom and sides. Baste the pocket in place along the top and side edges, about ⅛" in from the edges. How you divide the pockets is up to you, but for mine I stitched down the vertical center and 10½" in from each side, marking the stitching line with a light pencil mark or an air-soluble pen. This makes four pockets, about 10" wide, which seems perfect for things like a box of wipes, diapers, and children's books.

Start your stitching at the top edge of the pocket, sew forward and backward across the top where the fabrics meet, and then sew straight down the line and off the edge of the fabric. Alternatively, you can do a zigzag at the top edge for a more secure pocket as described in "Patch Pockets" on page 93.

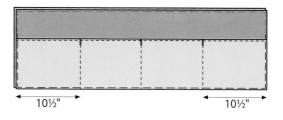

4. Attach the Ties

Fold the remaining body piece in half along the long edges, and finger-crease the fold at the top edge. Fold each ribbon length in half crosswise. Center one ribbon tie on the right side of the body fabric at the crease mark, aligning the fold of the ribbon with the raw edge of the fabric. In the same manner, pin a ribbon about ½" in from each end. Center and pin a ribbon between each end ribbon and the center ribbon. Baste the ribbons in place, about ⅛" from the top edge of the body piece. Fold the ends of the ribbon ties up and pin them to the body somewhere near the center so they won't get sewn into the seams later.

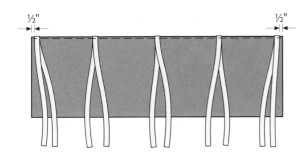

5. Sew the Backing Together

Lay the back piece over the pocket piece. Stitch around all of the edges, leaving an opening along the bottom for turning.

6. Finish Your Organizer

Turn the organizer right side out, using a point turner to push out the corners. Press the seams, folding under the seam allowance along the opening. Pin the opening closed, and then topstitch about ⅛" from all of the edges, closing the opening at the same time. Tie the ends of each ribbon in a knot and run a bead of seam sealant along the raw edge to keep it from fraying.

7. Hang Your Organizer

To hang your organizer in a crib, simply tie the ribbons together over one of the rails. To hang the organizer on the wall, paint your dowel with your craft paint and foam paintbrush; let dry. Then, tie each tie in a bow on the dowel so that they all hang at the same length. Position the dowel on the wall, and hammer three or four nails under the dowel to secure.

You're done! Now go organize some changing supplies.

Diaper Stacker

I thought diaper stackers were weird, until we bought a fold-up crib for a trip and a diaper stacker came with it. I used it on the trip, loved it, and started using it at home as well. It wasn't the most attractive thing in the world, so I made one that matched Presley's room. Even if you think these things are as weird as I did, give this one a try. It's a quick, inexpensive project, and I bet you'll like it as much as I like mine. Commercially made versions seem to either tie onto something or hang from a hanger. I made this one so it can do both. Either tie it on the end of your crib or changing table, or tie it to a hanger and hang it from a doorknob or hook. Either way, when made with a charming print, this will add to the cute (and organized) factor in your nursery!

FINISHED SIZE
12" x 20" x 8"

SKILL LEVEL

Easy

MATERIALS

Yardage is based on 42"-wide fabric.

⅝ yard of main print for front, back, and base

½ yard of contrasting print for sides, top, front-opening binding, and ties

½" bias-tape maker (optional)

12" x 18" piece of plastic canvas to stabilize base

PATTERN NOTES

- All seam allowances are ¼" and are included in the cutting dimensions.
- Wash, dry, and iron all fabrics before cutting out the pieces.
- I chose not to line this piece because I wanted it to be quick and inexpensive to make.

CUTTING

From the main print, cut:
1 strip, 17½" x 42"; crosscut into:
    1 rectangle, 12½" x 17½"
    2 rectangles, 6½" x 17½"
    1 rectangle, 8½" x 12½"

From the contrasting print, cut:
2 rectangles, 8½" x 17½"
2 rectangles, 3½" x 12½"
2 strips, 2" x 42"; crosscut into:
    2 strips, 2" x 18"
    4 strips, 2" x 16"

INSTRUCTIONS

Sew all pieces right sides together using a ¼" seam allowance unless otherwise noted. Refer to "Seam Finishes" on page 94 for seam-finishing options.

1. Make the Ties and Front-Opening Binding

Follow the bias-tape maker instructions to make bias tape from the contrasting-print 2" x 16" and 2" x 18" strips, or, if you're not using the bias-tape maker, refer to step 1 of "Topstitched Double-Fold Binding" (page 91) to press each strip in half and then press the long edges to the center. Set aside the longer strips for the front-opening binding. Open one end of each of the shorter strips and fold one short end of each strip ¼" to the wrong side. Refold the binding. Topstitch about ⅛" from the short and long folded edges.

2. Attach the Binding to the Front Pieces

Refer to "Topstitched Double-Fold Binding" to bind one long edge of each main-print 6½" x 17½" rectangle. With right sides up, butt the two bound edges together and baste across them along the top and bottom edges of the opening.

Baste.

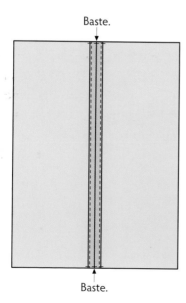

Baste.

3. Assemble the Body

With the long edges aligned, pin and then sew the contrasting-print 8½" x 17½" rectangles to the sides of the front piece. Press the seam allowances open. Pin and then sew the remaining long edges of the side pieces to the main-print 12½" x 17½" rectangle. Press the seam allowances open. If you're using a directional print, be sure all of the prints are going in the same direction.

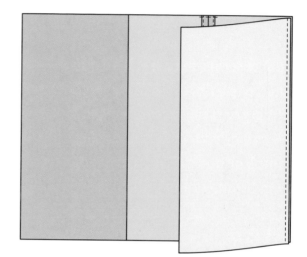

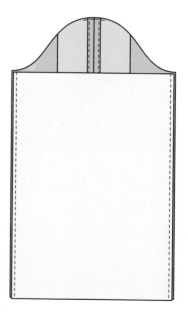

4. Attach the Base

Find the centers of the front, back, and side pieces of the body by folding each in half vertically. Finger-crease the folds at the bottom edge of all of the pieces, as well as at the top edge of the side pieces. Fold the main-print 8½" x 12½" rectangle in half vertically and horizontally and finger-crease the folds at each edge to mark the centers. With the body and bottom centers and corners aligned, sew the bottom to the body, stitching across the opening a couple of times to reinforce the seam.

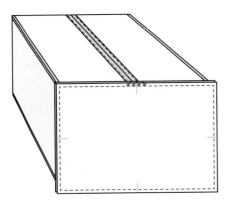

5. Create the Topper

Stack two of the ties you made in step 1 on top of each other, raw edges aligned. With the raw edges aligned, pin them to the right side of one long edge of a contrasting-print 3½" x 12½" rectangle, 1½" in from one side. Repeat on the opposite side with the remaining two ties. Baste the ties in place, about ⅛" from the edge. Place the remaining contrasting-print 3½" x 12½" rectangle over this rectangle and sew the pieces together along the short sides and the long side with the ties attached.

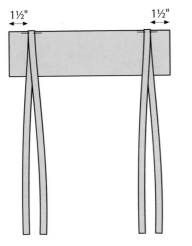

6. Create the Side Pleats

Turn the body piece right side out. At the top edge on one side, bring the front and back side seams together so they meet at the center of the side piece to form a pleat. Baste the pleat in place ⅛" from the raw edge. Repeat on the opposite side.

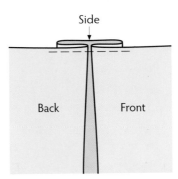

7. Attach the Topper

Turn the body wrong side out. Drop the topper, right side out and tie side down, into the top opening of the body and align the raw edges. Matching the side seams on the topper to the side seams on the body, use a generous amount of pins to pin the pieces together. Sew around the topper, sewing over the front opening a couple of times to reinforce the seam.

8. Finish the Stacker

Cut the plastic canvas into two 8" x 12" pieces and stack them on top of each other. Glue or stitch them together at the corners. Drop this piece into the base of the stacker to give it structure. Remove this piece when washing the stacker.

You've now got a finished stacker. Go stack some diapers!

Hooded Towel

We bought a couple of those little triangular hooded towels before my son Presley was born, and they worked for, like, two months. After that I kicked myself every bath time for buying them because they just didn't work; they weren't big enough. I went to replace them with the bigger toddler/kid-sized towels and was shocked at the price. I had one I liked from Ikea and realized one bath time that it would be simple as pie to replicate. So I did, and bought the supplies for about 25% of the purchase price of most of the ones I was seeing. The best part? It's mega quick to make. And? It will last as long as your munchkin uses hooded towels. Depending on if you use your towels more than once before washing, I recommend making three to five of these guys to keep by the tub.

FINISHED SIZE
One size fits 3 months and older

SKILL LEVEL

Easy

MATERIALS

Yardage is based on 42"-wide fabric.

1½ yards of solid-color terry cloth

½ yard of coordinating cotton print for binding

PATTERN NOTES

- All seam allowances are ½" and are included in the cutting dimensions.
- Wash, dry, and iron all fabrics before cutting out the pieces.
- Though not required, a walking foot will make it much easier to keep the layers from shifting as you sew them together.

CUTTING

From the terry cloth, cut:
1 piece, 27" x 50", from the *lengthwise* grain
1 piece, 13" x 18"

From the cotton print, cut:
Enough 3"-wide bias strips to make approximately 200" of bias binding

INSTRUCTIONS

Sew all pieces right sides together using a ½" seam allowance unless otherwise noted.

1. Make the Binding

Referring to steps 1 and 2 of "Topstitched Double-Fold Binding" (page 91), use the 3"-wide bias strips to make single-fold bias tape, folding the long edges in to the center. You will need one piece that's approximately 160" long and another that is approximately 36" long.

2. Make the Hood

Fold the terry-cloth 13" x 18" piece in half to make a 9" x 13" piece. Sew one short side together to create the seam at the top of the hood. Zigzag or serge the edges of the seam allowances to keep them from fraying. Press the seam allowances to one side. Turn the hood right side out.

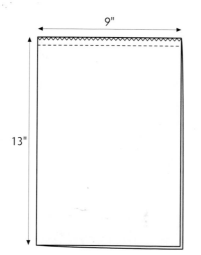

3. Bind the Hood

Refer to "Topstitched Double-Fold Binding" to bind the front raw edges of the hood with the 36"-long bias-tape length you made in step 1, leaving the unseamed edge unbound. Trim any excess binding even with the edges of the hood.

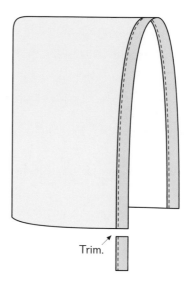

Trim.

4. Join the Hood to the Body

Fold the terry-cloth 27" x 50" piece in half along one long edge and pin-mark the fold. Fold the raw edge of the hood in half and pin-mark the fold. With the pin marks aligned, baste the hood in place, about ¼" from the edges.

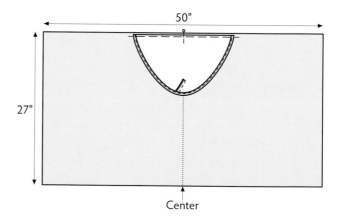

Center

5. Attach the Binding to the Towel

Refer to "Topstitched Double-Fold Binding" to bind the towel raw edges, catching the hood raw edge in the binding across the top of the body.

6. Finish the Hood

Lay the towel on your ironing board with the inside facing up and the hood folded upward. Press the seam that attached the hood to the body toward the hood; pin it in place. From the right side, topstitch along the seam on the hood side of the towel, catching the binding. Run a second line of topstitching just above the first line to secure the hood in place.

Go turn on the water—it's bath time!

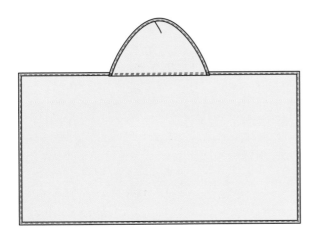

⊙ THEME TIME!

If you don't want to just bind your towel with a print that matches your nursery theme, think about adding ears, or eyes, or a tail, or whatever you want to the towel. It's really easy to stitch some extra fabric to the hood and give your towel a personality.

Super Bib!

It's a bib! It's a bandanna! It's a fashion statement! You'll love this. I mean it. I found a ready-made bib-danna when Presley was 18 months old and kicked myself for not having sought out one sooner. I'd have used this every day of his first year if I'd had it, so I knew I needed to include my own version here. Apparently, I was blessed with a barfy baby. We went through so many burp cloths when he was little, and I changed his shirt about 10 times a day because it was always wet from drool and spit-up. Regular bibs looked dorky and never stayed put for long. This one, though, rolls up around the neck, creating lots of surface area to catch liquids. Had I had this cool bib, he'd have been a little cowboy all the time and I'd have cut my laundry in half. Make a dozen of these; you won't regret it!

FINISHED SIZE
One size fits about 3 months and older

SKILL LEVEL

 Super Easy

MATERIALS

Yardage is based on 42"-wide (or wider) fabric. Fat quarters are approximately 18" x 21".

⅜ yard of terry cloth (any width) for bib back

1 fat quarter *OR* ⅜ yard of contrasting quilting cotton or flannel for front

1 fat quarter of contrasting quilting-cotton print for binding

2 sets of size 4 sew-on snaps

Hand-sewing needle and matching thread

PATTERN NOTES

◆ The bib pattern is on pullout pattern sheet 2.

◆ All seam allowances are ¼" and are included in the pattern.

◆ Wash, dry, and iron all fabrics before cutting out the pieces.

◆ Instead of buying terry cloth by the yard, I bought a hand towel to make my sample.

CUTTING

From *both* the bib front and back fabrics, cut:
1 bib piece

From the binding fabric, cut:
Enough 2"-wide bias strips to make approximately 44" of bias binding

Super Bib! in multiple colorways

INSTRUCTIONS

1. Sew on the Snaps

Using a needle and matching thread, sew the snaps to the front and back bib pieces where indicated on the pattern. You'll be sewing the male half of one snap to the front of the bib and the female half of both snaps to the back of the bib. Having two snaps will allow the bib to be adjusted as your kiddo grows.

2. Baste the Front and Back Together

Pin the bib pieces wrong sides together. If needed, trim the pieces so they match. Baste the pieces together, about ⅛" from all of the edges.

3. Attach the Binding

Referring to "French Double-Fold Binding" (page 90), use the 2"-wide bias strips to make and attach the binding to the bib edges.

Put your Super Bib! on a super baby!

NURSERY SEWING BASICS

To help you get started, I've covered the basics you'll need to know to make all the projects in this book.

FABRIC TYPES

Though I love just about everything to do with sewing, I can definitely say the fabrics are my favorite part. Color and texture and prints together make me a very happy person.

Quilting Cottons

This is the main type of fabric I used in this book. Quilting cottons are widely available everywhere from specialty quilt shops to major chain stores to online shops, in a huge range of colors and prints. The best way to pick your quilting cottons is to feel the fabric for quality. Scratchier cottons are generally lower quality and will not wear as well, and wearing well is important for baby items that will be washed 100 million times! I used organic quilting cottons for the majority of my projects in this book, because I like to think my baby items are as safe for sensitive little ones as possible, and they feel heavier and nicer to me than many other options available.

Fleece

I used polar-fleece-type fabric for a couple items in this book. Fleece is washable, snuggly for baby, perfect for toys, and easy to work with because it sticks to itself and the edges don't fray. It's available in a huge range of colors and prints and very easy to find at fabric stores, major chain stores, and online shops. I have found most fleeces are pretty hard wearing for lots of washing, but if you go with the slightly higher-priced ones at the major chain stores, the extra dollar or two a yard you pay will be made up for many times over in durability.

Cotton Jersey Knit

Cotton jersey knit is just about my favorite baby fabric. I used it for so many projects when I sewed for my son Presley. Though you can generally find it fairly easily in a wide range of solid colors, it can be a little tough to find in cute prints. If you keep your eyes open and do a little searching on the Internet, particularly in Etsy.com shops, you can sometimes hit the jackpot. When buying jersey at a major chain store, I choose my jersey by holding up a single layer and checking if I can see through it. The less I can see through it, the thicker and better quality it is. Though I didn't use jersey for many projects in this book, you can sub it in for just about everything. No need to be afraid of sewing it either; a ballpoint needle and a straight stitch on your machine will do the trick. Just make sure not to stretch it as you sew!

Some of the fabrics used in this book, from left to right: two examples of quilting cotton, fleece, cotton jersey knit, ultra-plush fleece, and terry cloth

Plush Fabrics

I used synthetic ultra-plush fleece, such as Minky, on several projects. These fabrics can be a big pain to work with because they shed all over the place when you cut them, but they sure make a nice finished item for babies and toddlers, so I find them worth the mess. These fabrics are unbelievably soft and snuggly. They're available in a wide range of colors, prints, and textures, and they're fairly easy to find at local fabric stores and big chain stores, as well as online.

Terry Cloth

I used terry cloth for several projects for this book, but it can be hard to find in a wide range of colors and prints. Instead of shopping at the fabric store for terry cloth, I recommend hitting a big-box store or discount store for towels. The less expensive towels tend to be thinner, which makes them easier to sew with.

Canvas and Heavyweight Fabrics

I only used canvas on the "Mei Tai Baby Carrier" (page 51), but it's a must to hold up to carrying a baby around. When looking for a sturdier-weight fabric like this, look for the fabrics called "bottom weights," or you could even check in the home-decorating-fabrics department. These types of heavier fabrics stand up fairly well on their own and would be great to sub in for projects like the "Diaper Stacker" (page 73) or "Soft Toy Bin" (page 19) where you're creating something with structure. Just check the washing instructions on the fabric and make sure to find something that will hold up to those 100 million washings.

 THEMES!

I'm really into themes. Like *really* into themes. Because of this, some of the projects in this book include one version in a basic patterned print and one "theme" version using fabrics with things like rocket ships and farm animals on them. If you've decided on a theme for your nursery, I hope these themed samples will help you pick fabrics that incorporate either the colors or images of your decided theme.

Rocket ships and space

Bright geometric patterns

PREPARE YOUR FABRIC

Whatever fabric you pick for your project, be sure to wash it before you start sewing with it. Washing your fabric will mean any shrinking or color bleeding will happen before you've put all the time and energy into making it into something. I also prewash my batting to decrease the amount of shrinking once my project is finished, but this isn't recommended for all batting types, so check the package for prewashing instructions. I tend to wash my fabrics, no matter what type, on my washer's gentle, cold-water setting to keep them from fraying too much. Then I dry them in the dryer on a low setting and remove them right away when the dryer is done to prevent wrinkles.

Once your fabric is washed and dried, be sure it's free of major creases and wrinkles. I tend to iron all of my fabric with a steam setting and the appropriate temperature for the fabric after washing it to make it nice and flat before cutting.

WHERE TO FIND FABRICS

Fabric shopping is the best! This is where you get to pick your own colors and patterns and really make these projects your own.

Local fabric and quilt shops. Though going to a big chain fabric store may seem like the easiest route, I encourage you to find your local fabric and quilt shops and check them out for fabric first. They tend to stock better-quality fabrics in a wider range of colors and prints. There is one local craft-store chain out of three or four total stores in my area that I just love. Though they have fewer options than a major chain, I always come away from there with the "perfect" choice for my projects, whereas at the big chain store I tend to settle with something that will be just "OK." And supporting local shops supports the crafters in your area, rather than a big, faceless retail corporation.

Online. I love the Internet for fabric shopping. Though I really like to be able to feel my fabrics and see the colors in person before purchasing, the amazing variety of unusual and unique fabrics available online make up for that for me. There are tons of online fabric shops (fabricworm.com being my favorite), but I encourage you to check out all the fabric and supply sellers on Etsy.com as well. You can be really specific with your search terms on Etsy if you have something special in mind, or do a broad search by simply searching "fabric." Either way, one of my favorite parts of online shops (especially Etsy shops) is that the majority are small businesses, so your purchases are supporting little independents.

IT'S WHAT'S INSIDE THAT COUNTS

Sometimes you need more than just a beautiful fabric to make your project complete.

Interfacing

Interfacing is used when you need to give your fabric a little more structure than it has on its own. There are a ton of options out there. The best way to pick one is to feel the weight of many kinds, keeping in mind the weight of the fabric you're using it with and what you want the final product to feel like. I always buy the fusible types because I find them the easiest to use. When I need more structure, like for the "Soft Toy Bin" (page 19), but I don't want the "crunchy" feeling a heavy-duty interfacing can sometimes create, I use craft felt. I buy 72"-wide yardage, because it's very inexpensive. Then I use it as interfacing between the layers of fabric to give my project a sturdier shape.

Batting

I feel completely confused every time I walk down the batting aisle of the fabric store. There are so many fiber contents and other options, I never know what to pick. For some of the projects, I mentioned what type of batting I used, so you can feel a little less confused walking into the store. If you have a batting you like to use, feel free to go with that one rather than my suggestion.

BASIC TOOL KIT

Having the right tools makes sewing way more enjoyable. In the following pages you'll find the basics you need to make all of your projects a success. You'll need the same basic set of tools for all of the projects. Be sure you have the following on hand when you sit down to start your project.

The Heart of Your Sewing Room: Your Sewing Machine

Your sewing machine is your most important tool for any sewing project. The most important things to keep in mind when picking your sewing machine are that you should love it and that you will oil and clean it regularly. Honestly, I have sewn on everything from a $20 garage-sale find to a $2500 industrial machine, and the biggest factor in sewing-machine performance is maintenance so you enjoy sewing on it. It doesn't need to be fancy-pants or expensive, it just needs to go forward and backward and do a straight and zigzag stitch. Just be sure to give it a try to see how you get along before you buy a machine, and then read the manual and know when and how to oil it. It is also helpful to take it for a checkup with your local sewing-machine repair shop every year or so, even if you don't sew on it much. Actually, machines that sit around and gather dust tend to be in the most need of a checkup!

Straight to the Point: Sewing-Machine Needles

There are several types and sizes of sewing-machine needle, so choose the best one for your fabric, taking the type of thread into consideration as well. Needles get dull, so be sure to change your needle regularly. I change mine after about every eight hours of sewing, or you could change it at the start of every new project. If you're having stitching issues, the first thing to do is change the needle. You will be surprised how much it helps!

Sharp needles have a sharp point designed to penetrate woven fabrics. Use a Sharp needle for anything woven like cotton, canvas, terry, or woven fleece (many are knit). Sharps are particularly good for topstitching and other decorative stitching.

Ballpoint needles have a rounded point designed to push between the yarns of a knit fabric, rather than going through them like sharp needles do. Use ballpoint needles when you're sewing any type of knit fabric, like jersey, interlock, or knit fleece.

🔘 BASIC TOOL KIT CHEAT SHEET

Here are some examples of the basic tools you'll want to keep on hand:

1. standard presser foot;
2. walking foot; 3. zipper foot; 4. assorted sewing-machine needles; 5. rotary cutter; 6. assorted thread in neutral colors; 7. thread snips; 8. fabric shears; 9. glass-head pins; 10. bent safety pins.

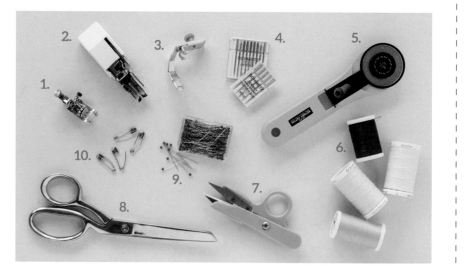

Jeans or denim needles are sharp needles with heavy-duty shafts designed to sew through thicker materials or multiple layers of material. These are good to use on projects with multiple layers like the "Soft Toy Bin" (page 19).

Universal needles are a combination of sharp and ballpoint needles, designed to penetrate woven materials but rounded enough to push between the fibers of a knit. Because they are not designed for either specifically, I find they sew neither well. Avoid universal needles, unless they're the only option.

Under Pressure: Presser Feet

Most sewing machines have a plethora of presser feet available. The projects in this book use three specific types.

Standard foot: This is the foot that generally comes on the machine. The standard foot will be open in the middle, making it good for sewing a straight stitch, a zigzag stitch, or decorative stitches. You'll use this foot the most.

Zipper foot: This is a narrow foot that allows you to sew right up next to things, like when attaching a zipper. Your sewing machine will most likely come with a zipper foot. In the projects in this book, you'll use it on a couple projects where you attach a zipper, but it's also good for sewing things like piping.

Walking foot: A walking foot is a special foot used mainly for quilting. The foot has its own set of feed dogs that move in conjunction with the feed dogs on your sewing machine. With both sets of feed dogs working, the top and bottom layers of fabric move at the same speed. It's particularly handy when sewing a thicker project like a blanket with batting in it; a regular presser foot has the tendency to push the batting at a different speed than the fabric, causing it to bunch. Though generally fairly easy to find, walking feet can be pricey. It just depends on the brand. The walking foot for one of my sewing machines costs $150, whereas the walking foot for another costs $13. This foot is not required, but it will make your life much, much, much easier on several of the projects in this book.

String It Together: Thread

Be sure to pick a high-quality thread for all of your projects. I've had the best luck with all-purpose thread from Coats & Clark and Gütermann. Though you'll need to match your thread to your project for topstitching or sewing appliqués, you can use a neutral thread like white, black, khaki, or gray for doing general construction. Using a neutral color for construction will cut down on how many thread changes you need to do, which is always a plus!

Be Sharp: Cutting Tools

There are many ways to cut your fabric. Always keep a high-quality, sharp pair of **scissors** (fabric shears) on your cutting table and a small set of **thread snips** by your sewing machine. I use my thread snips for ripping stitches rather than a seam ripper, so I make sure to have a pair with a nice, sharp point to get into stitches. Be sure to get your scissors sharpened regularly too!

Rotary cutter: My favorite tool in my sewing room, aside from my machine, is my rotary cutter. It's a must for not only quick cutting, but super-straight and accurate cutting. Be sure to use it on a **self-healing mat**, and run the blade of the rotary cutter along a **metal or clear acrylic ruler** for the best results. I refrained from putting a picture of my scarred finger in here, but be super diligent about keeping your hands away from the blade.

Hot, Hot Heat: Ironing

Be sure to have a good-quality **iron** with steam settings. You can also use a spray bottle filled with water to mist your fabric for a similar effect, but you really want a steam iron. Be sure if you haven't used your iron in a while to test it on a scrap of fabric and make sure it hasn't rusted when using water in it.

You'll also need an **ironing board**, full-sized or tabletop depending on how much space you have. I recommend a full-sized board, even if you're tight on space, because it just makes the job easier. I know it can take up a huge amount of space—my sewing room and office while writing this book was about 100 square feet—but it can double as an extra table in a pinch, and it folds down flat when not in use.

Hold It Together: Pins

Be sure you have lots of **pins** for your projects! I use long, straight, glass-head pins for all of my projects. Though glass-head pins tend to cost a little more, it's worth it if you accidentally leave one in and iron over it, because you won't melt the head. I store my pins on a magnetic pincushion so that when I'm sewing and toss one in the general direction of the cushion, the magnet helps to keep it in place. If you find a pin that's bent, throw it out! Bent pins are too hard to work with, and it's not worth trying to straighten them. They've done their job, and it's time for them to go.

Another handy type of pin I've found in the last year is the **bent safety pin** (they're bent *on purpose*). Though I didn't specifically call for them in this book, and they aren't 100% necessary, they're helpful on any blanket project that involves pinning multiple layers of fabric and batting together.

TECHNIQUES

Rather than repeating common techniques in every project, I've put together some of the basic techniques I've used in this section so I can go into a little more depth. Even if you consider yourself an expert sewist, this is a good section to review to see how I do things. Who knows, you might learn something new!

Pressing Seams

When a pattern calls for you to "press" a seam, place your iron on the seam, applying gentle pressure. Don't move the iron around like you do when ironing out wrinkles or you'll distort the seam.

⊙ LINE IT UP

Many patterns call for you to press under an edge to the wrong side anywhere from ¼" to ¾". You can use one of those little adjustable rulers made for this type of task, but I find them annoying, and they get hot when using them with an iron. If you want to go for cheap and easy like I do (always things I look for as a mama), take a piece of scrap paper or four-squares-to-the-inch graph paper and draw lines ¼", ½", and ¾" from the straight edge. Then just run the piece of paper along the edge of the fabric, fold to the line, and press. Easy.

Putting in a Zipper

Several projects in this book call for zipper closures. A couple of them use a different method, but here's a general technique for inserting a zipper between two pieces of fabric.

1. With right sides facing, line up the edge of the zipper with the edge of one of your fabric pieces that the zipper will be between.

2. Using your zipper foot, position the needle to sew right next to the zipper. Sew along the zipper, lining up the edge of the foot with the edge of the fabric. Backstitch at the beginning of the seam.

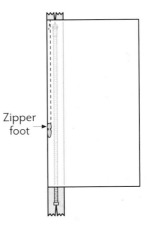

Zipper foot

3. Fold the fabric back so the right side is facing up and press along the seam. Topstitch along the fold of the fabric.

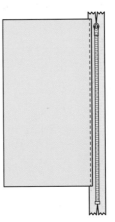

4. Repeat steps 1–3 with the remaining fabric piece on the opposite side of the zipper.

Making and Applying Bias Binding

Some of the projects in this book use bias-tape binding to finish raw edges. This is a simple and effective technique that I love because it allows me to add a small amount of extra color or print to my project. I apply my binding using two different techniques: French double-fold binding and topstitched double-fold binding. You can buy binding premade, but it's so easy to make it yourself, and making it allows you more options and colors to match your project. You can also purchase a bias-tape maker, which is a little metal tool you slide your fabric through to create the folds, but it's not absolutely necessary. There are only a few sizes of these available and some of the projects in this book use unusual sizes of bias binding. Here's how to make and apply it yourself.

JOINING BINDING STRIPS

If you need to create a piece of binding that's longer than one cut strip, here's how to join the strips.

Place the ends of two strips right sides together at a 90° angle, overlapping the ends. Using a pencil and ruler, draw a line from the inside point where the strips intersect to the outside point where the strips intersect. Pin the strips together. Sew on the line, backstitching at the beginning and end of the seam. Trim ¼" from the stitching line. Press the seam allowances open. Repeat with any remaining strips to make the strip the length you need.

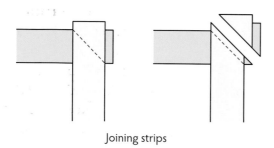

Joining strips

Press seam open.

FRENCH DOUBLE-FOLD BINDING

1. Press your binding strip in half lengthwise, wrong sides together.

2. Starting at about the middle of one side of the project, lay the strip on the project, lining up the raw edges; pin the strip in place along that side. Beginning several inches from the end of the strip, sew the binding in place using the seam-allowance width called for in your project instructions. Stop stitching a seam-allowance width from the corner; backstitch.

Seam allowance width

Front

3. Fold the binding strip up at a 90° angle from the corner to create a 45°-angle fold in the binding. Keeping the fold intact, fold the binding strip back down, aligning the raw edges with the next side to be stitched. Starting at the fold, backstitch, and then sew to within a seam-allowance width of the next corner. Repeat the folding and stitching process with the remaining sides and corners.

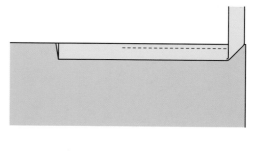

4. When you are several inches from the start of the binding strip, stop sewing; backstitch.

5. Overlap the binding ends the width of the binding strip. For example, if your binding strip is 2" wide, overlap the binding ends 2". Trim the excess binding strip.

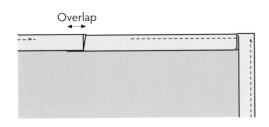

6. Open up the binding strips and place the ends at right angles to each other. Refer to "Joining Binding Strips" on page 90 to mark a diagonal line across the strip. Stitch on the marked line. Check to make sure the binding fits along the remainder of the edge, and then trim ¼" from the stitching line. Press the seam allowances open.

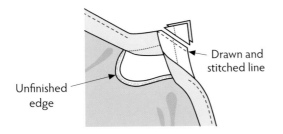

7. Refold the binding and continue stitching it in place, backstitching at the beginning and end of the seam line.

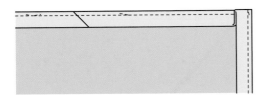

8. Fold the binding over to the back of the project so that it covers the stitching line. Pin the binding in place, mitering the corners.

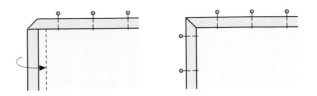

9. From the right side, topstitch around the project, about ⅛" in from the edge of the binding, catching the edge of the binding on the back. As you come to the corners, put your needle down into the piece and pivot the piece so you're set up to sew down the next side. Backstitch your seam at the beginning and end of the binding.

TOPSTITCHED DOUBLE-FOLD BINDING

For this method, you sandwich the edge of the fabric is between the two layers of binding and then topstitch it in place. Easy peasy! When you're working with fabric binding, the edges are folded under to the wrong side first to finish them, but if you're working with satin blanket binding, like in the "Pocket Blanket" (page 63), the ribbon edge is finished so it won't unravel, so all you have to do is sandwich your fabric between the binding and topstitch.

1. Press the binding strip in half lengthwise, wrong sides together. Unfold the binding and then press the long edges to the wrong side the amount indicated in the project. For some projects, you'll fold the edges to the center; for others, only ½" will be folded under. Make sure you check your project for specifics, and refer to "Line It Up" (page 89) for an easy way to measure your folds.

2. Fold the strip in half again, aligning the folded edges.

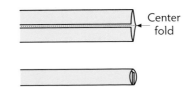

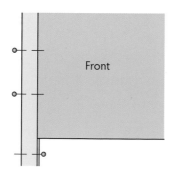
3. Starting at about the center of one edge, sandwich the project edge between the binding folds; pin in place along one side. When you come to the corner, bring the binding straight down from the corner and place a pin in the binding the finished binding strip width away from the corner. So, if your binding finishes at ½", place a pin ½" from the corner—through the top layer of binding only.

4. Open up the tape and turn the corner by matching up the pin with the edge of the tape, creating a 45° angle on the back of the project. Then, fold the tape in half around the edge, creating a 45° angle on the front of the corner as well. Remove the pin and use it to secure the corner in place. Continue pinning the binding to the edges, mitering the corners as you go.

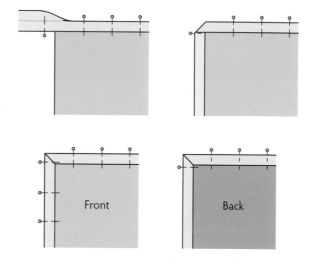

5. When you get to the beginning of the binding, overlap the ends 1", trimming the excess. Fold under the raw end ½" and wrap the binding over the edge, enclosing the raw end at the beginning of the binding; pin in place.

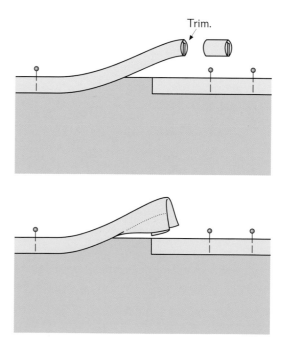

6. Topstitch around the binding, about ⅛" from the inside folded edge, backstitching at the beginning and end.

Patch Pockets

Several projects have patch pockets, which I like because they are super simple to make and attach. Here's how I make them. Use the seam-allowance width called for in the project instructions, and backstitch whenever you start and end a seam.

1. Fold the pocket piece in half, right sides together, so you have three sides that are approximately the same length.

2. Sew each side seam. For the last seam, opposite the folded edge, sew a few inches and then backstitch. Without cutting the thread, lift the presser foot and needle and begin stitching 3" to 4" from where you ended.

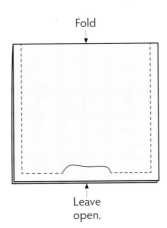

Fold

Leave open.

3. Turn the pocket right side out through the opening. Press the pocket flat, making sure the seam allowances of the opening are pressed to the inside of the pocket.

4. Topstitch about ¼" from the top folded edge.

5. Pin the pocket to your piece according to the project instructions. Begin sewing at one side of the topstitched edge, using a medium-width, short-length zigzag stitch. Zigzag for ¼" to ½", backstitch, and then continue stitching down the side of the pocket using a medium-length straight stitch. Pivot at the bottom corner, stitch across the bottom, pivot at the opposite corner, and then stitch toward the folded edge, switching back to a zigzag stitch ½" to ¼" from the top edge.

That's it! Zigzagging like this at the beginning and the end will make your pocket corners more secure.

Ladder Stitch

Although I close the openings on the seams of most of my projects with the machine, occasionally there's one that needs to be finished by hand. To do this, use any type of hand-stitching needle and a thread that matches your fabric. Though you can use a quick-and-dirty finish like a whipstitch, I prefer to use an invisible seam if I'm taking the time to do it by hand. My preferred invisible closure is a ladder stitch.

1. Press under the seam allowances along the opening edges and pin them in place. Anchor your knot in the underside of the seam allowance on one side of the opening and bring the needle out through the folded edge.

2. Insert the needle through the opposite folded edge, run it down about ¼", and bring it out the same folded edge.

3. Insert the needle through the opposite fold directly across from where you brought your needle out, run it through the edge about ¼", and bring the needle out of the fold.

4. Continue in this manner back and forth through the folded edges, gently pulling the thread as you go to close up the gap. You'll see the bars of the "ladder" begin to appear between the two folds.

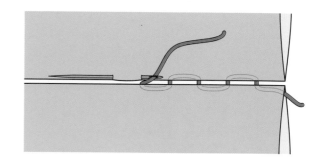

5. Anchor the thread at the other end by sewing several small stitches on top of each other, and then snip off the excess thread.

Seam Finishes

To keep your seams from raveling and to just give your project a neater appearance, it's a good idea to finish the edges of your seam allowances. There are several ways to do this, but these three options generally work well for most of the projects in this book.

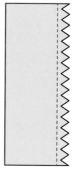 

Pinked   Zigzag   Serged
                stitched

RESOURCES

Please check your local fabric and quilt shops for the materials needed to sew the projects in this book. The following companies generously donated the materials to make the samples shown throughout these pages.

Birch Fabrics
Organic fabrics
www.birchfabrics.com

Monaluna
Organic Fabrics
www.monaluna.com

Moda
Quilting cottons
www.unitednotions.com

Riley Blake
Quilting cottons, cotton jersey, jumbo pom-pom trim
www.rileyblakedesigns.com

Pellon
Interfacing, stuffing, quilt batting
www.pellonprojects.com

American Felt and Craft
Squeakers, rattle inserts, crinkle material, bells, and more
www.americanfeltandcraft.com

ACKNOWLEDGMENTS

A huge thank-you to everyone for making this book possible. I love writing, and it is such a big thrill that I am able to write my fourth book and first-ever sewing book! So cool.

- To the folks at Martingale, thank you for believing in me again.
- To my agent, Linda, thank you again for being so amazing.
- To Mr. Danger and my two Master Dangers, you guys sure are an awesome family!
- To my family, thanks for the continued support and encouragement.
- Thank you to the baby models and their moms for their time.
- Thank you again to all of the companies for so generously donating the supplies in this book.

ABOUT THE AUTHOR

Rebecca Danger *is a craft-pattern designer who lives in Lake Stevens, Washington, with her husband, Mr. Danger; their sons, Presley and Maverick; and their two pugs, Abbey and Lucy— plus a whole menagerie of knitted and sewn toys. She's got a great blog at www.rebeccadanger.typepad.com and a monster of a website at www.dangercrafts.com.*

Rebecca believes that crafting is a lifestyle, not just a hobby. Because she really, really, really likes to knit, she started knitting rather obsessively and writing patterns for her original toy designs in February of 2009. She's written more than 100 published knitting patterns to date, including three successful knitting books. With a background in sewing, Rebecca also started writing a few sewing patterns, which has led to this, her first sewing book. She really likes being able to craft for work since it means she gets to knit and sew all day, tell the government that all of her yarn and fabric purchases are business expenses, and still be able to afford to feed her family.